Armstrong's Essential Skills for People Professionals

Armstrong's Essential Skills for People Professionals

A complete guide for HR practitioners

Michael Armstrong

KoganPage

First published in Great Britain and the United States in 2024 by Kogan Page Limited

2nd Floor, 45 Gee Street
London
EC1V 3RS
United Kingdom

8 W 38th Street, Suite 902
New York, NY 10018
USA

4737/23 Ansari Road
Daryaganj
New Delhi 110002
India

www.koganpage.com

Kogan Page books are printed on paper from sustainable forests.

ISBNs

Hardback   978 1 3986 1477 2
Paperback   978 1 3986 1476 5
Ebook   978 1 3986 1478 9

British Library Cataloguing-in-Publication Data
A CIP record for this book is available from the British Library.

Library of Congress Control Number
2024932498

Typeset by Integra Software Services, Pondicherry
Print production managed by Jellyfish
Printed and bound by CPI Group (UK) Ltd, Croydon, CR0 4YY

CONTENTS

PART THREE Analytical, technical
and research skills

Introduction: the nature of skill

This book is about the wide variety of skills that people professionals need to carry out their job. A skill is basically the ability to do something well in order to put into practice the requirements of a role. Exercising skill means applying relevant knowledge and making the best use of natural or acquired abilities. So this book is concerned with role requirements for the knowledge and ability associated with skill as well as with the skills themselves.

The meaning of skill

Skill is a learned ability to apply knowledge effectively in performing a role or task. It is knowing how to do something and then doing it. Skill is developed through the acquisition of knowledge and experience. Skills are the basis for getting work done and are transferable.

Hard skills are the technical or manual skills required to do a job. Soft skills are mainly concerned with interpersonal relationships involving interactions between people. Skills make use of knowledge – the theoretical or practical understanding of a subject. They can be abstract, e.g. analytical skills, or concrete – the capacity to do what is necessary to fulfil the demands of a role by carrying out the tasks involved effectively. The successful performance of a role requires appropriate abilities as well as knowledge and skills. Abilities are natural or innate and are harder to teach, test or measure.

The acronym KSA (knowledge, skills and abilities) provides a framework for defining generally what people at work need to know and be able to do, and specifically for defining role requirements (role profiles), person specifications for recruitment purposes, and learning specifications setting out learning and development needs.

People management skills

The skills used by people or HR professionals will depend on their role as examined in part one (Chapter 1) of this book. They are summarized in Chapter 2. The skills are described in more detail in the remaining parts as follows:

Part 2 covers 'process skills'. These are the skills needed to carry out the fundamental activities or processes of people management.

Part 3 covers analytical and critical skills such as problem solving, critical and systems thinking, the use of statistics and conducting research.

Part 4 covers the personal skills needed to carry out fundamental people management processes and handle people management issues.

Part 5 covers the skills required to handle people problems, conduct challenging conversations, function in a political context and manage conflict.

Part 6 addresses the need for people professionals to be business-like, including the administrative and project management skills required.

PART ONE
People management skills: the framework

The role of people management

People management is concerned with the development and application of good people practice and with the successful exercise of the skills required. It is necessary to understand what the roles of the people management (HR) function and people management (HR) professionals are before examining those skills. This is done in this chapter under the following headings:

1 Role of the people management function

2 People management activities

3 Organization of the people function

4 Role of the people management professional

5 Tips

Role of the people management function

Peter Cheese, the Chief Executive of the Chartered Institute of Personnel and Development (2021), summed up its role as follows:

> The people management function does not manage the people (apart from within the function), but they are there to understand the needs of the people and the business, to provide the insight and the changes and interventions that need to happen, and to enable, to guide, to support, and to ensure compliance where it is needed.

IES research (Brown et al., 2019) defined the role as being there to display:

> 'a real understanding of the business and working with senior leaders' combined with 'the ability to identify and prioritise people issues… and help managers to see practical solutions to their people problems'.

Dave Ulrich (1998) made the following point in his influential *Harvard Business Review* article:

> HR should not be defined by what it does but by what it delivers – results that enrich the organization's value to customers, investors, and employees.

People management activities

The activities of the people management function can be divided into three areas: transformational, transactional, and concern for the organization's values and social responsibility.

Transformational

Transformational activities are those that make a significant difference for the organization or for its employees. The people management function provides expertise and insight to explore new ways of meeting current and future challenges. It enables the organization to achieve its goals by developing people strategies and delivering advice and services in accordance with good practice in each aspect of people management. It contributes to the formulation and implementation of corporate strategy and helps the organization to succeed in ways that lay the foundations for future, sustainable success by taking steps that will improve individual and therefore organizational performance.

As Lawler and Mohrman (2003) commented:

> HR can play an important role in the formulation of strategy by making explicit the human capital resources required to support various strategies and strategic initiatives, by playing a leadership role in helping the organization develop the necessary capabilities to enact the strategy, and by playing a strong role in implementation and change management.

In the words of Ulrich (1998), HR should be 'an agent of continuous transformation'.

Transactional

Transactional activities consist of the basic services that the people function is there to deliver effectively and efficiently. The main areas of service delivery are: recruitment, talent management, learning and development, reward management, employment relations, employee wellbeing, dealing with day-to-day people issues, and employee records. The people function also ensures compliance with the provisions of employment law.

Concern for the organization's values and social responsibilities

People professionals have a special responsibility for guarding and promoting core values in the organization on how people should be managed and treated and how their wellbeing is catered for. They need to take action to achieve fair dealing and equal opportunities. This means treating people according to the principles of procedural, distributive, social and natural justice, and seeing that decisions or policies that affect them are transparent in the sense that they are known, understood, clear and applied consistently. Kochan (2007: 600) suggested that:

> HR derives its social legitimacy from its ability to serve as an effective steward
> of a social contract in employment relationships capable of balancing and
> integrating the interests and needs of employers, employees and the society in
> which these relationships are embedded.

Organizations have a social purpose and this should be fostered by the people management function. It means the exercise of social responsibility – an ethical framework which indicates that individuals and organizations should work and cooperate with each other for the benefit of society at large. It is concerned with sustainability – the need to develop environmental, social and economic policies that take into account their future impact and provide for this impact to be maintained.

Organization of the people function

The operating model for the organization of the people management function varies depending on the context of the organization – its size, the extent to which operations are decentralized, the type of work carried out, the kind of people employed and the role assigned to the function. As Peter Cheese (2021) observed: 'The operating model for HR should be whatever best fits the business.'

A survey by the CIPD (2022a) found that there were two prominent operating models adopted by UK people teams: a business partnering model with specialists and shared services (30 per cent), and having a single HR team that includes generalists, specialists and administration all together (31 per cent). The notion of organizing people management into three major areas, what the CIPD calls the business partnering model, sometimes also referred to as the three-stooled model, emerged from the HR delivery model produced by Ulrich (1998). The areas are: (1) business partners who work closely with line managers to help them fulfil their responsibilities, (2) centres of expertise that specialize in the provision of high-level advice and services on key people management activities such as talent management, learning and development and reward, and (3) shared service centres that provide 'transactional' services across the business such as recruitment, absence monitoring and advice on dealing with employee issues.

Role of the people management professional

People management professionals provide advice, guidance and services on all matters concerning the employment of people. They can act as strategists, business partners, innovators or internal consultants. Their roles vary considerably.

The CIPD (2013) defined the people profession as 'an applied business discipline with a people and organization specialism'. The CIPD's Profession Map (2022b) states that:

> The fundamental purpose of the people profession is to champion better work and working lives. Creating roles, opportunities, organisations and working environments that help get the best out of people, delivering great organisational outcomes, in turn driving our economies, and making good, fair and inclusive work a societal outcome.

The roles of people professionals vary according to the extent to which they are generalist (e.g. people director, people manager, people business partner, people officer), or specialist (e.g. head of learning and development, head of talent management, head of reward). They also change in line with the level at which they work (strategic, executive or administrative), the needs of the organization, the view of senior management about their contribution, the context within which they work and their own capabilities.

Dave Ulrich (1998) suggested that HR specialists can function in four ways: as a strategic partner, an administrative expert, an employee champion and a change agent. This model was later modified by Ulrich and Brockbank (2005), who defined five roles:

1 *Employee advocate* – focuses on the needs of employees through listening, understanding and emphasizing.

2 *Human capital developer* – focuses on preparing employees to be successful in the future.

3 *Functional expert* – concerned with the HR practices that are central to HR value on the basis of the body of knowledge they possess.

4 *Strategic partner* – combines the multiple dimensions of business expert, change agent, strategic HR planner, knowledge manager and consultant to align HR systems to help accomplish the organization's vision and mission, helping managers to get things done and disseminating learning across the organization.

5 *Leader* – leading the HR function, collaborating with other functions and providing leadership to them, setting and enhancing the standards for strategic thinking and ensuring corporate governance.

They commented on the importance of the employee advocate role, noting that people professionals spend about one-fifth of their time on employee relations issues and that caring for, listening to and responding to employees remains a centrepiece of their work. The Ulrich model draws attention to the multi-faceted and therefore multi-skilled nature of the role, although most attention has been paid to the notion of the strategic nature of the work and the concept of the strategic business partner.

How people management professionals carry out their roles depends on the context in which they work (the size and culture of the organization, the types of activities it carries out, the type of people employed and the requirements of senior management), their skills and disposition and, importantly, the values they adopt. They will be affected by questions on the status of the profession and what is involved in being a professional. It can be a difficult job to do well and the criteria for success are demanding.

The activities and roles of people management specialists and the demands made upon them as described above appear to be quite clear cut but this is often not the case, and Thurley (1981) pointed out that they were specialists in ambiguity. Their situation has not changed significantly since then.

The difficulties that people professionals face in dealing with ambiguity were well described by Guest and King (2004):

> Much management activity is typically messy and ambiguous. This appears to apply more strongly to people management than to most other activities. By implication, the challenge lies not in removing or resolving the ambiguities in the role [of people professionals] but in learning to live with them. To succeed in this requires skills in influencing, negotiating and learning when to compromise. For those with a high tolerance of ambiguity, the role of HR specialist, with its distinctive opportunity to contribute to the management of people in organizations, offers unique challenges; for those only comfortable if they can resolve the ambiguities, the role may become a form of purgatory.

Keegan and Francis (2010) came to the following conclusions on the basis of their research:

> Bearing in mind the history of HR practitioners' struggles for acceptance as key organizational players it is hardly surprising that a way of discursively modelling the concept of HR as 'hard' and relating it to other concepts such as 'business-driven agendas' and 'strategic management' has become so popular. It offers perhaps a way out of the dualism when they seek to claim a share of strategic decision making while at the same time struggling to attend to the employee-centred and administrative aspects of the role.

TIPS

- Be clear about the role of the people management function. Achieve an appropriate balance between its transformational and transactional roles.
- Get to know the business or corporate strategy of the organization and its business or operational goals. Work out what people management strategies should be developed to contribute to the achievement of these goals.
- Demonstrate as far as you can just how people management policy and practice make that contribution.
- Do what you can to ensure that the organization's approach to people management is value-driven and that its social purpose is achieved.

- Develop a mix of generalist and specialist knowledge and expertise, always bearing in mind the strategic direction and needs of the organization and the character and needs of employees and line managers.

- Establish a balanced and productive partnership relationship with line managers. Balance devolving responsibility for operating people management processes to line managers with the need to ensure that policy guidelines are followed and people management decisions are fair and consistent.

- Practice an open, transparent and engaging approach to people management. Involve line managers and employees directly and as early as possible in diagnosing current needs and priorities and discussing any changes under consideration. Hold regular forums to gauge their needs, views and reactions.

- Establish clear criteria for the performance and success of the people management function. Monitor, regularly report on and evaluate people management policies and decisions, and advise senior leaders and line managers on alternative approaches and improvements as necessary.

References

Brown D, Hirsh W and Reilly P (2019) Strategic human resource management in practice: case studies and conclusions – from HRM strategy to strategic people management, Institute for Employment Studies, https://www.employment-studies.co.uk/system/files/resources/files/Strategic-Human-Resource-Management-in-Practice.pdf (archived at https://perma.cc/E62W-QXFC)

Chartered Institute of Personnel and Development (2013) *HR Profession Map*, London, CIPD

Chartered Institute of Personnel and Development (2022a) *People Profession Survey*, London, CIPD, https://www.cipd.org/uk/knowledge/reports/people-profession-survey/ (archived at https://perma.cc/8UCS-NSA2)

Chartered Institute of Personnel and Development (2022b) People Profession Map, London, CIPD, https://www.cipd.org/globalassets/media/comms/the-people-profession/profession-map-pdfs/profession-map_full-standards-download.pdf (archived at https://perma.cc/63XH-WT34)

Cheese, P (2021)*The New World of Work*, London, Kogan Page

Guest, D E and King, Z (2004) Power, innovation and problem-solving: the personnel managers' three steps to heaven? *Journal of Management Studies,* **41** (3), pp 401–23

Keegan, A and Francis, H (2010) Practitioner talk: the changing textscape of HRM and emergence of HR business partnership, *The International Journal of Human Resource Management,* **21** (6), pp 873–98

Kochan, T A (2007) 'Social legitimacy of the HRM profession: a US perspective', in (eds) P Boxall, J Purcell and P Wright, *The Oxford Handbook of Human Resource Management,* Oxford, Oxford University Press, pp 599–619

Lawler, E E and Mohrman, S A (2003) What does it take to make it happen? *Human Resource Planning,* **26** (3), pp 15–29

Thurley, K (1981) Personnel management: a case for urgent treatment, *Personnel Management,* August, pp 24–29

Ulrich, D (1998) A new mandate for human resources, *Harvard Business Review,* January–February, pp 124–34

Ulrich, D and Brockbank, W (2005) *The HR Value Proposition,* Cambridge, MA, Harvard Press

The skills of people management professionals

02

The considerable range of skills required by people professionals are examined in this chapter under the following headings:

1 Role requirements of people professionals
2 Skill requirements
3 Tips

Role requirements of people professionals

Research conducted by Brockbank et al. (1999) led to a definition of what they called competency 'domains', as set out in Table 2.1.

Research by the Institute for Employment Studies (Brown et al., 2019: 56) concluded that the capabilities of people management professionals consist of:

> ... a real understanding of the business and ability to work closely with senior leaders; the ability to identify and prioritise people issues; understand the timeframes on which they need to be addressed; and help managers to see practical solutions. This sometimes means challenging the views of senior people and reminding them of the importance of taking a customer and employee perspective, not just seeing the business from their own point of view.

A survey of people professionals by the CIPD (2022) revealed that the considerations shown in Figure 2.1 were the ones that most concerned the 1,496 respondents.

Table 2.1   Key HR specialist competency areas

Competency domain	Definition
1 Personal credibility	Live the firm's values, maintain relationships founded on trust, act with an 'attitude' (a point of view about how the business can win, backing up opinion with evidence).
2 Ability to manage change	Drive change: ability to diagnose problems, build relationships with clients, articulate a vision, set a leadership agenda, solve problems and implement goals.
3 Ability to manage culture	Act as 'keepers of the culture', identify the culture required to meet the firm's business strategy, frame culture in a way that excites employees, translate desired culture into specific behaviours, encourage executives to behave consistently with the desired culture.
4 Delivery of human resource practices	Expert in the specialty, able to deliver state-of-the-art innovative HR practices in such areas as recruitment, employee development, compensation and communication.
5 Understanding of the business	Strategy, organization, competitors, finance, marketing, sales, operations and IT.

It is interesting to note that a number of the considerations, including the most important one, were concerned with relationships between people professionals and their line managers and other colleagues; also that building specialized prestige is given the next-to-lowest priority.

People management professional behaviours CIPD

The CIPD Profession Map (2021) states that members of the people profession should be 'principles led, evidence-based, outcomes driven'. The map sets out the following core behaviours expected of people professionals:

- *Ethical practice* – Building trust by role-modelling ethical behaviour, and applying principles consistently in decision making. People professionals should be value driven.

Figure 2.1   Areas for improvement in HR capabilities

Supporting line managers in their people management roles	▬▬▬▬▬▬	39%
Using data to inform decision making	▬▬▬▬	27%
More flexible working collaboration with colleagues	▬▬▬▬	27%
Working collaboratively with colleagues	▬▬▬▬	25%
Demonstrating HR's roles to line managers as credible business partners	▬▬▬	17%
Developing confidence to challenge and influence other areas of the business to prioritize people considerations	▬▬▬	16%
Building specialized expertise	▬▬▬	16%
Building commercial business knowledge and acumen	▬▬	12%

SOURCE Adapted from Chartered Institute of Personnel and Development (2022) *People Profession Survey*, London, CIPD

- *Professional courage and influence* – Showing courage to speak up and skilfully influencing others to gain buy-in; taking a stand with colleagues when it is the right thing to do despite significant opposition or challenge.
- *Valuing people* – Creating a shared purpose and enabling people development, voice and wellbeing.
- *Working inclusively* – Working and collaborating across boundaries, effectively and inclusively, to achieve positive outcomes.
- *Commercial drive* – Using a commercial mindset, demonstrating drive, and enabling change to create value.
- *Passion for learning* – Demonstrating curiosity and making the most of opportunities to learn, improve and innovate.
- *Insights-focused* – Asking questions and evaluating evidence and ideas to create insight and understand the whole.
- *Situational decision making* – Making effective and pragmatic decisions or choices based on the specific situation or context.

Skill requirements

All people professionals need to use to a greater or lesser extent interpersonal, analytical, insight, agility, communications, business, professional, managerial and administrative skills. The precise nature and extent of these will vary according to their role and context.

Interpersonal skills

People management professionals spend much of their time interacting with other people, within and outside the organization. They use interpersonal skills to provide advice and guidance, to exert influence and leadership, to deal with people problems, to cope with political situations and to manage change and conflict.

Analytical skills

Analytical skills are deployed to gain a better understanding of the factors affecting decisions about a course of action or the approach to dealing with a people management issue or problem. They are used when sorting out the different aspects of complex situations and their relative significance as part of a system. This requires the ability to visualize, articulate and solve complex problems and make decisions based on logical and critical thinking and evidence. This ability is crucial to people professionals constantly faced with the need to gain insight into the organizational and business issues they have to address.

Agility skills

Agility in people management was defined by the CIPD (2011) as:

> The ability to stay open to new directions and be continually proactive, helping to assess the limits or indeed risks of existing approaches and ensuring that leaders and followers have an agile and change-ready mindset to enable them and ultimately the organisation to keep moving, changing, adapting.

Organizational insight

The CIPD (2010) commented on the importance of organizational insight as follows:

> Organizational insight is the juxtaposition of a deep understanding of what will help make your organization successful – or stop it from being so – in the market within which it operates at this stage in its evolution, together with a deep appreciation of what goes on around here and what really make things happen here (given people, politics and culture). The former derives from understanding the key drivers of the business, the wider market and the context in which it sits. The latter comes from the 'intelligence' generated both systematically through data gathering and analysis, as well as from the discrete activities and interactions HR engages in across the organization.

An HR executive reported by the CIPD (2010) commented that:

> We need deep employee insights – not just employee engagement surveys which just scratch the surface. As an HR function we need a deep and segmented understanding of employees' aspirations, motivations and needs in some ways akin to how a customer-facing company thinks about its customers.

Communication skills

People professionals need communication skills to persuade management and line managers to accept their proposals and advice and to keep employees informed on developments that affect them. They must be able to clearly present to management information assembled through people analytics on what is happening in their organization as it affects people management policy and practice.

Business skills

In their role as business partners supporting the achievement of the business goals of the organization, people professionals need business skills. They need to understand the business model and business strategy of the organization in order to create integrated people management strategies. People professionals can also contribute to enhancing organizational performance in their capacity as performance consultants and individual performance by developing ways of motivating and engaging employees and promoting a learning culture.

Professional, managerial and administrative skills

People professionals need to have the professional skills required in each aspect of people management to provide the advice and services that will further the interests of stakeholders – the organization, employees and the public at large. The main areas covered by the advice and services are organization development, resourcing, talent management, learning and development, reward management, managing diversity and promoting inclusion, employee benefits and wellbeing, and the achievement of the social purpose of the organization. They also have to be able to exercise leadership and administer the people management services efficiently.

TIPS

- Analyse your role as a people management professional and identify the skills you need to carry it out successfully.
- Consider the extent to which you have the skills required.
- Decide what you need to do to remedy any deficit.

References

Brockbank, W, Ulrich, D and Beatty, D (1999) HR professional development: creating the future creators at the University of Michigan Business School, *Human Resource Management*, **38**, Summer, pp 111–17

Brown, D, Hirsh, W and Reilly, P (2019) Strategic human resource management: case studies and conclusions: from HR strategy to strategic people management, Institute for Employment Studies, https://www.employment-studies.co.uk/resource/strategic-human-resource-management-practice-case-studies-and-conclusions (archived at https://perma.cc/GV8U-SMMH)

Chartered Institute of Personnel and Development (2010) *Next Generation HR: Time for change: towards a next generation for HR*, London: CIPD

Chartered Institute of Personnel and Development (2011) *Shaping the Future*, London, CIPD

Chartered Institute of Personnel and Development (2014) HR: Getting smart about agile working, https://www.cipd.org/globalassets/media/knowledge/knowledge-hub/reports/hr-getting-smart-agile-working_2014_tcm18-14105.pdf (archived at https://perma.cc/P7WW-ULK3)

Chartered Institute of Personnel and Development (2021) People Profession Map, London, CIPD, https://www.cipd.org/uk/the-people-profession/the-profession-map/explore-the-profession-map/ (archived at https://perma.cc/SL2R-8KJF)
Chartered Institute of Personnel and Development (2022) People Profession Survey, London, CIPD, https://www.cipd.org/uk/knowledge/reports/people-profession-survey/ (archived at https://perma.cc/W23Z-AXC2)

PART TWO
People management process skills

Strategic people management skills 03

People management professionals have a strategic role when they take part in conjunction with management and their line manager colleagues in the development and implementation of innovative people strategies that support the achievement of the organization's strategic goals. In this chapter the strategic management skills required by people professionals are examined under the following headings:

1 The strategic role of people professionals
2 The nature of strategy and strategic management
3 How people professionals carry out their strategic role
4 The strategic business partner model
5 Tips

The strategic role of people professionals

Taking a strategic view and developing integrated people strategies is an essential aspect of the role of the head of a people management department, but adopting a strategic approach and using strategic management skills is also an important part of the work of anyone in charge of a major people management function such as learning and development, and of those who take on the role of business partner. In its profession map, the CIPD (2022) emphasized that people professionals should understand how 'to identify strategic opportunities and adapt people strategies for a hybrid workforce' and know their organization's 'strategy, priorities and issues, and how these connect to people strategy and people priorities'.

The nature of strategy and strategic management

Before considering the strategic skills needed by people professionals it is necessary to examine the nature of strategy and strategic management.

Strategy

The classic definition of strategy was made by Chandler (1962) who wrote that it was 'The determination of the long-term goals and objectives of an enterprise, and the adoption of courses of action and the allocation of resources necessary for carrying out those goals.' Boxall and Purcell (2016) suggested that 'Strategies are the ways in which managers of firms understand their goals and develop resources – both human and non-human – to reach them. Some strategies may be formally planned but it is inevitable that much of a firm's strategy emerges in a stream of action over time.' A businessman's view on strategy was made by Julian Richer (2017) who defined it as simply the process of 'identifying the direction we should be moving in'.

Strategy has three fundamental characteristics. First, it is forward-looking. It is about deciding where you need to go and how you mean to get there. In this sense a strategy is a declaration of intent: 'This is what we want to do and this is how we intend to do it'. Strategies define longer-term goals but they also cover how those goals will be attained. They guide purposeful action to deliver the required result. A good strategy is one that works, one that, in Abell's (1993) phrase, ensures that organizations adapt to changing demands and circumstances by 'mastering the present and pre-empting the future'. As Boxall (1996) explained: 'Strategy should be understood as a framework of critical ends and means.'

The second characteristic of strategy is the recognition that the organizational capability of a firm (its capacity to function effectively) depends on its resource capability (the quality and quantity of its resources, especially people, and their potential to deliver results). This is called the resource-based view.

The third characteristic of strategy is that it aims to achieve strategic fit. This is the need when developing functional strategies such as people management to achieve congruence between them and the organization's business strategies within the context of its external and internal environment and also to ensure that the different aspects of people strategy cohere.

Strategic management

As stated by Boxall and Purcell (2016): 'Strategic management is best defined as a process. It is a process of strategy making, of forming and, if the firm survives, reforming its strategy as the environment changes.' Strategic management was described by Johnson et al. (2005) as 'understanding the strategic position of an organization, making strategic choices for the future, and turning strategy into action'. The purpose of strategic management was expressed by Kanter (1984) as being to 'elicit the present actions for the future and become action vehicles – integrating and institutionalizing mechanisms for change'.

The key strategic management activity identified by Thompson and Strickland (1996) is 'deciding what business the company will be in and forming a strategic vision of where the organization needs to be headed – in effect, infusing the organization with a sense of purpose, providing long-term direction, and establishing a clear mission to be accomplished'. Truss et al. (2012) emphasized the action-oriented nature of strategic management. They defined it as 'the process that enables organizations to turn strategic intent into action'.

The focus is on identifying the organization's mission and strategies, but attention is also given to the resource base required to make it succeed. Managers who think strategically will have a broad and long-term view of where they are going. But they will also be aware that they are responsible first for planning how to allocate resources to opportunities that contribute to the implementation of strategy, and second for managing these opportunities in ways that will add value to the results achieved by the organization.

How people professionals carry out their strategic role

People management activities support the achievement of the organization's goals and values by aligning people strategies with business or corporate strategies. People professionals share responsibility with their management colleagues for the success of the organization. A key aspect of the role of senior people management professionals is to practise strategic management by getting involved in the development and implementation of forward-looking people strategies that are integrated with the business strategy and one another. Importantly, they work with their line management colleagues in the continuous formulation and execution of the business strategy.

Taking into account the people management implications

People management professionals, especially at the higher levels, make a strategic contribution that ensures that the organization has the quality of skilled and engaged people it needs. Sparrow et al. (2010) observed that 'HR must be fully responsive to the strategy and business model of the business. HR is not a rule to itself. It is not "HR for HR", but HR (as broadly defined across the competing stakeholders whom HR has to satisfy) for the business.' The strategic nature of HR has been expressed in the strategic business partner model, as described below.

The strategic business partner model

People management practitioners can be described as strategic business partners when they have the capacity to identify business opportunities, to see the broad picture and to understand how their role can help to achieve the organization's business or corporate objectives. They integrate their activities closely with those of top management and line managers. They anticipate needs, act flexibly and are proactive. In effect, they say to their colleagues, 'We know you're going places and we're going to help you get there'.

TIPS

- Think about what the organization wants to be and become and what needs to be done to ensure that this happens.
- Gain and maintain insight into the real needs of the business and its people.
- Take a broad view of where the business is going.
- See 'the big picture', looking beyond the confines of the immediate problems faced by the business and its people to what lies ahead and how these problems can be solved.

- Contribute to the formulation of business and corporate plans.
- Advise on the people management implications of business plans and issues.
- Engage in systemic thinking to gain understanding of how to align the different elements of the organization's system (for example, the values, culture, structures, people practices and policies) to maximize the organization's performance.
- Develop and apply business, problem-solving, systems thinking and analytical skills.

References

Abell, D F (1993) *Managing with Dual Strategies: Mastering the present, pre-empting the future*, New York, Free Press

Boxall, P F (1996) The strategic HRM debate and the resource-based view of the firm, *Human Resource Management Journal*, **6** (3), pp 59–75

Boxall, P F and Purcell, J (2016) *Strategy and Human Resource Management*, 4th edition, Basingstoke, Palgrave Macmillan

Chandler, A D (1962) *Strategy and Structure*, Boston, MA, MIT Press

Chartered Institute of Personnel and Development (2022) People Profession Map, London, CIPD, https://www.cipd.org/uk/the-people-profession/the-profession-map/explore-the-profession-map/ (archived at https://perma.cc/8R5A-4PWB)

Johnson, G, Scholes, K and Whittington, R (2005) *Explaining Corporate Strategy*, 7th edition, Harlow, FT Prentice Hall

Kanter, R M (1984) *The Change Masters*, London, Allen & Unwin

Richer, J (2017) *The Richer Way*, London, Business Books

Sparrow, P, Hesketh, A, Hird, M and Cooper, C (2010) Introduction: Performance-led HR, in P Sparrow, A Hesketh, M Hird, and C Cooper (eds) *Leading HR*, pp 1–22, Basingstoke, Palgrave Macmillan

Thompson, A A and Strickland, A J (1996) *Strategic Management: Concepts and cases*, 9th edition, Chicago, Irwin

Truss, C, Mankin, D and Kelliher, C (2012) *Strategic Human Resource Management*, Oxford, Oxford University Press

Business partnering skills 04

The notion of people management professionals working in conjunction with line managers as business partners has become familiar since it was originated by Dave Ulrich in 1998. This chapter deals with the skills required under the following headings:

1 The business partner role
2 The partnership role of people management professionals
3 Tips

The business partner role

When people professionals act as business partners they work alongside their line management colleagues in order to develop and implement a people management agenda that contributes to achieving the business or corporate goals of the organization or function. They share responsibility with their line management colleagues for the success of the latter's function or department, and get involved with them in implementing the business or corporate strategy. They may be 'embedded' in an operational division or department or be part of a centralized people management function. The CIPD (2022) explained that the role of business partners was to 'align with business leaders to enhance workforce performance, foster and nurture strategic people enablers such as talent, leadership, learning and culture, as well as develop people solutions, to achieve organisational objectives'. Ulrich and Beatty (2001) stated that the strategic business partner 'represented a "player" whose aim is to add value through acting as a "coach, architect, builder, facilitator, leader and conscience"'.

The partnership role of people management professionals

It is not just business partners who need to adopt a partnering approach with line managers. This applies to all people management professionals. Partnership means working with line managers to deal jointly with people issues and, importantly, implementing people strategies and new people policies and practices. Traditionally, some people management specialists have tended to lay down the law to their line manager clients: 'This is the policy, this is what you have to do about it, this is how I am going to help you.' In a partnership mode, they will still explain what the policy is and what the responsibilities of the manager are in implementing it, and they will still provide guidance and advice. But in adopting a partnership approach the people professional will focus on understanding the particular preoccupations and concerns of individual managers and working alongside them to produce a joint agreement on how to proceed based on that understanding. It will be a matter of agreeing rather than prescribing.

When acting as partners, people specialists have to demonstrate to line managers that they understand the situation in which the latter operate and the pressures they face. People management professionals need to be appreciated as colleagues who know about the business and will listen to managers when they make suggestions or express doubts about a new policy. They will discuss possible approaches and agree modifications to fit particular circumstances as long as these do not fundamentally affect the policy. They will work alongside line managers when a new policy is being introduced, not as a prescriptive trainer but, in effect, as a coach.

The following practical advice on carrying out the role was given by two strategic business partners in a London-based US investment bank, interviewed by Pritchard (2010):

- 'I think the way you change their [the business clients'] behaviours in the longer term is by getting to be a trusted advisor, and the way to become a trusted advisor is to know your individual, to know your client and to know how to hook the individual.'

- 'If you don't know the little things, they'll [the business leaders] never trust you with the bigger things… you survive by doing the little things and doing them right, and then building up that trust and that relationship with them.'

TIPS

- Understand the business as a whole and its competitive environment.
- Understand the goals of their part of the business and its plans to attain them.
- See the broad picture of how the people management function can contribute to business success.
- Ensure that their activities support the strategic activities of their colleagues.
- Build relationships with their line manager colleagues founded on trust and demonstrated expertise.
- Be proactive, anticipating requirements, identifying people issues and problems and producing innovative and evidence-based solutions to them that are aligned with business requirements.
- Respond to the needs of managers and ensure that the transactional people management services required by them are provided by colleagues in central or shared services departments, by themselves or by outsourcing.

References

Chartered Institute of Personnel and Development (2022) Business Partnering, London, CIPD, https://www.cipd.org/uk/knowledge/factsheets/business-partnering-factsheet/ (archived at https://perma.cc/MDQ4-46RU)

Pritchard, K (2010) Becoming an HR strategic partner: tales of transition, *Human Resource Management Journal*, **20** (2), pp 175–88

Ulrich, D (1998) A new mandate for human resources, *Harvard Business Review*, January–February, pp 124–34

Ulrich, D and Beatty, D (2001) From partners to players: extending the HR playing field, *Human Resource Management*, **40** (4), pp 293–307

Organization development skills

05

Organization development interventions aim to improve the effectiveness with which organizations function. People professionals play an important part in encouraging management to support such interventions and in managing them. The skills required are considerable. This chapter is set out under the following headings:

1 The nature of organization development

2 The skills required

3 Tips

The nature of organization development

Organization development was defined by the CIPD (2022) as 'a planned and systematic approach to enabling sustained organizational performance through the involvement of its people'. Its aims and characteristics are as follows:

1 It is concerned with an organization's strategy, goals and core purpose.

2 It focuses on maximizing the value gained from the organization's resources.

3 It applies behavioural science knowledge and practice, such as leadership, group dynamics and work design, to improve the extent to which competitive advantage is delivered through the people in the organization.

4 It takes the form of a planned, ongoing, systematic change activity that aims to institutionalize continual improvement within the organization.

The skills required

According to the CIPD (2022), organization development practitioners should have:

> expertise in navigating complexity to unpick what the organization is trying to achieve; diagnose underlying issues, challenges, opportunities; and select the best approaches to develop the organization moving forward... They should leverage their expertise and knowledge of the organization to question assumptions, help surface non-obvious problems/issues, diagnose barriers and enablers of execution, and manage change effectively.

To put organization development into practice requires specific analytical, diagnostic, change management and facilitating skills.

Analytical skills

Analytical skills as described in more detail in Chapter 7 are used to gain understanding of a complex situation by breaking it down to its constituent but inter-related parts. They provide a way to gain insight into the issues that affect the success of the organization and which influence business or corporate and people management strategy.

Diagnostic skills

Diagnostic skills are used to identify and define problems in order to solve them. A diagnosis is based on the analysis of evidence assembled to illuminate the features of the situation. Specially developed diagnostics can be used for this purpose, consisting of checklists or questionnaires that are constructed on the basis of research and provide information on the nature of a situation or process – for example, the *Organizational Culture Inventory* devised by Cooke and Lafferty (1989). Other diagnostics such as SWOT and PESTLE examine the circumstances and performance of the organization within the context of its business and social environment. The Environmental, Social and Governance (ESG) framework used by the City to evaluate the performance of businesses has recently emerged as a valuable analytical and diagnostic tool that has direct links to how the business community regards a firm.

Diagnostic skills comprise the abilities required to identify the significant features of a situation, to select the most appropriate ways to understand the nature of that situation, e.g. the choice of diagnostics, and to draw conclusions on the basis of that evidence. This could lead to a prognosis – a prediction of what will happen if nothing is done about the problem – and in the light of that prognosis and the supporting evidence, a decision on the action that needs to be taken.

Change management skills

Change management involves such activities as identifying the need to change, consulting people on what should be done about it, involving them in planning and implementing the change, communicating the details of the change, spelling out how it will work, why it is necessary and how they will be affected by it, and ensuring that the people, mechanisms and infrastructure needed to implement the change are available.

Facilitation skills

Facilitation skills are those required to encourage cooperation and achieve consensus. They involve active listening, awareness of others and their behaviour, and helping people to understand what they need to do.

TIPS

- Remember that organizations can be more effective if they learn to diagnose their own strengths and weaknesses.
- Bear in mind that managers often do not know what is wrong and can benefit from help in diagnosing problems, although the aim is always to ensure that decisions are made by the managers themselves.
- Develop work system processes, practices and policies to enable employees to perform to their full potential. This may include the establishment of a high-performance work system (HPWS) or focusing on lean manufacturing, smart working or the enhancement of levels of engagement.
- Promote the use of business process modelling techniques to obtain insight into the business issues facing the organization and lead to plans for practical interventions that address those issues
- Use interactive skills training techniques to improve the ways in which people in teams work together.

References

Chartered Institute of Personnel and Development (2022) Organization Development, London, CIPD, https://www.cipd.org/uk/knowledge/factsheets/organisational-development-factsheet/ (archived at https://perma.cc/G87A-NWL6)

Cooke, R and Lafferty, J (1989) *Organizational Culture Inventory*, Plymouth, MI, Human Synergistic

Change management skills

06

People professionals are frequently involved in introducing new policies and practices. This is not always easy and change management skills are needed to do it, as described in this chapter under the following headings:

1 The process of change management

2 The role of people professionals in managing change

3 The skills required to manage change

4 Tips

The process of change management

Change management is about ensuring that change happens in a considered way with the maximum degree of acceptance and the minimum amount of disruption. Leading and facilitating change is a systematic process for initiating and achieving continuous improvement and the smooth implementation of new developments and initiatives.

The process of change

The process of change involves moving from a present state, through a transitional state, to a future desired state. Change can be gradual and unplanned, proceeding by incremental steps until it reaches the 'tipping point', the time when a trend spreads throughout the organization. The process of change management starts with an awareness of the need for change or that change is happening. An analysis of the present state and the factors that have created it leads to a diagnosis of the distinctive characteristics of the situation and an indication of how best the change can be managed. Possible courses of action can then be identified and evaluated and a choice made of the preferred action.

It is then necessary to decide how to get from here to there. This transitional state is a critical phase in the change process. It is here that the problems of introducing change emerge and have to be managed. These problems can include resistance to change, low stability, high levels of stress, misdirected energy, internal political pressures, conflict, and loss of momentum. Hence the need to do everything possible to anticipate reactions and likely impediments to the introduction of change. Kotter's 8-Step Change Model provides a useful guide.

Kotter's 8-step change model

The eight steps in the change model produced by John Kotter (1996) are:

1 *Establish a sense of urgency* – examine market and competitive realities. Identify crises and opportunities.

2 *Form a powerful guiding coalition* – assemble a group with enough power to lead the change effort and encourage it to work together as a team.

3 *Create a vision* – people must have a reason, and a really good one at that, for doing something different.

4 *Communicate the vision* – use every vehicle possible to communicate the new vision and strategies and teach new behaviours by the example of the guiding coalition.

5 *Empower employees* – leaders must clear the way for employees to develop new ideas and approaches without being stymied by the old ways.

6 *Create short-term wins* – plan and implement visible performance improvements.

7 *Consolidate improvements* – use increased credibility to change systems, structures and policies that don't fit the vision.

8 *Institutionalize new approaches* – anchor the changes in corporate culture.

Implementing change

It is usually not too hard to plan change. The real problem is to implement it. Lawler and Mohrman (2003) noted that:

> Implementation failures usually involve the failure to acknowledge and build the needed skills and organizational capabilities to gain support of the workforce, and to support the organizational changes and learning required to behave in new ways.

Research by Carnall (1991) in 93 organizations identified the following explanations for failures to implement change effectively:

- major problems that had not been identified beforehand emerged during implementation;
- coordination of implementation activities was not effective enough;
- competing activities and other crises distracted management from implementing the change decision;
- the capabilities of the employees involved were not sufficient;
- training and instruction to develop new skills was inadequate.

Implementation is likely to be more effective when the proposed change is practical, uncomplicated, can be put into effect without too much trouble and, importantly, there has been proper consultation with both managers and employees generally during the course of its development. Implementation may well be difficult if the change is detrimental to the interests of those affected by it, which means that every attempt should be made to justify it and mitigate any potential negative impacts. The aims should be to (1) keep it simple, (2) spell out *how* and *why* the change is to be implemented as well as *what* is to be implemented, (3) ensure that support is given to line managers in the shape of advice, guidance and training, and (4) 'hold the gains' provided for the benefits of the change to be maintained.

Resistance to change

People do not necessarily take kindly to change. It is quite naturally resisted when it is seen as a threat to familiar patterns of behaviour or to status and financial rewards. Resistance to change can be active when people take action to convey their hostility and stop or disrupt it. But when they are worried by change, they can respond passively by being unenthusiastic about its implementation and by subtly undermining change initiatives. The CIPD (2021) cited neuroscience research that showed that resistance may be a deep-rooted threat response, designed to keep us safe.

Resistance to change can be difficult to overcome, even when the change is not detrimental to those concerned. But the attempt must be made. The preliminary step is to analyse the potential impact of change by considering how it will affect people in their jobs and how they are likely to react. Managers and other employees should then be involved in the change process so that they can raise and resolve their concerns and make suggestions about the form of the change and how it should be introduced. The aim is to get 'ownership' – a feeling amongst people that the change is something that they are happy to live with because they have been involved in its planning and introduction – it has become *their* change.

The role of people professionals in managing change

Change is often initiated by senior management but the responsibility for implementing it mainly rests with line managers, advised and helped by people professionals. It was observed by Dave Ulrich (1997) that HR professionals should be 'as explicit about culture change as they are today about the requirements for a successful training program or hiring strategy'. He also emphasized that 'HR should become an agent of continuous transformation, shaping processes and a culture that together improve an organization's capacity for change'.

In its profession map, the CIPD (2022) stated that:

> People professionals are involved in all stages of change. We need business knowledge: how to build a case for change, develop costings and measures, and plan and deliver projects. But we also need an understanding of how to engage people for that change to be effective. How to choose the right approach that supports a change culture; how to involve the right people and listen to their views; how to continuously innovate and deliver change at pace, and knowing what else needs to be in place to enable that change for the long term.

The skills required to manage change

The wide range of skills required by people professionals to manage change are:

- *Insight* – understanding when and how change is taking place and the need to do something about managing it.

- *Analytical skills* – the ability to examine the nature of the change in order to decide what needs to be done, having taken into account the circumstances in which the change is taking place. Analytical skills are a means of gaining insight into any issues that will have to be dealt with.

- *Decision-making skills* – deciding what needs to be done by senior management, line managers and the people management function to facilitate change and overcome any resistance to it.

- *Influencing skills* – getting people (management, line managers and employees generally) to accept the need for change and agree on what needs to be done about it.

- *Communication skills* – the ability to communicate persuasively to all concerned what is happening or going to happen, why it is happening, the part they will pay and how they will be affected by it.

- *Facilitation skills* – in its broadest sense, facilitating involves the process of helping to make things happen. It means working out what new or different things people will have to know or be able to do to implement a change and providing them with the advice, guidance and specific training they therefore need.

TIPS

- Explain to stakeholders the reasons for change and how it will affect them.

- Make every effort to protect the interests of those affected by change.

- Remember that hard evidence and data on the need for change are the most powerful tools for its achievement, Evidence-based decisions are key to making organizational change successful. However, establishing the need for change is easier than satisfying it.

- Understand the culture of the organization and the levers for change that are most likely to be effective in that culture. Take account of the political pressures that may affect the achievement of change.

- Build a platform for change – a working environment that supports it.

- Accept that resistance to change is inevitable if the people concerned feel that they are going to be worse off – implicitly or explicitly. The inept management of change will produce that reaction.

- Get people to 'own' the change as something they want and will be glad to live with. People support what they help to create. Commitment to change is improved if those affected by change are allowed to participate as fully as possible in planning and implementing it.

- Bear in mind that change may mean the use of new skills and could be resisted because people are nervous about acquiring and applying them. Include training in any new skills as part of a change programme.

References

Carnall, C (1991) *Managing Change*, London, Routledge

Chartered Institute of Personnel and Development (2022) Profession Map, London, CIPD, https://www.cipd.org/uk/the-people-profession/the-profession-map/explore-the-profession-map/ (archived at https://perma.cc/V53H-WT2A)

Kotter, J P (1996) *Leading Change*, Boston, MA, Harvard Business School Press

Lawler, E E and Mohrman, S A (2003) HR as a strategic partner: What does it take to make it happen? *Human Resource Planning*, **26** (3), pp 15–29

Ulrich, D (1997) *Human Resource Champions*, Boston, MA, Harvard Business School Press

Skills analysis 07

People professionals are often called upon to analyse the skills required to carry out a role for a number of purposes. In this chapter skills analysis is covered under the following headings:

1 Skills analysis defined

2 Skills analysis techniques

3 Tips

Skills analysis defined

Skills analysis determines the skills used to achieve an acceptable standard of performance. It provides the basis for identifying learning needs, devising learning and training programmes and identifying skill requirements for recruitment purposes.

Skills analysis techniques

The basis of skills analysis is an understanding of the different types of skills that may be needed to carry out a role. These include:

- physical (manual) skills;
- administrative skills;
- digital skills;
- professional skills;
- the skills needed to follow complex procedures or sequences of activity;
- prioritizing and planning skills;
- leadership, people management and team-building skills;
- analytical, diagnostic, decision-making and problem-solving skills;
- communicating skills – written and oral.

It is also necessary to understand how these skills are typically learned and developed, for example through education, professional learning/training programmes, apprenticeships or internships, formal training courses, instruction, coaching or guidance from managers or colleagues, or simply by experience – picking up ways of doing things while carrying out work.

Skills analysis is based on information gained from managers or job holders. This is usually done in an interview during which the analyst finds out what the job holder has to know and be able to do in each of the main activity areas of the role.

This is not always easy. It takes skill to translate the sometimes incoherent and often incomplete information provided by managers and job holders. The analyst may have to probe to get useable information. This means having the skills required to interpret what they hear about the content of a job into a description of skill requirements. This process will be helped if the analyst knows the nature of the skills that are typically needed to carry out similar work. Knowledge of the content of educational or training programmes also helps.

TIPS

- Obtain information from job holders and their managers about what the job entails.

- Break down this information into the key result areas and establish what the job holder needs to know and be able to do in each area.

- Interpret the often incomplete or vague information about job content or skill requirements provided by managers or job holders in the light of your own knowledge of what these are in similar jobs.

- Obtain details of the skills developed through any education, training or experience job holders typically need to do the job.

Selection interviewing skills

08

A selection interview establishes the extent to which a candidate has the types and levels of knowledge, skills and abilities required to carry out a job. Because recruitment and selection is a major part of the work of a people management function, selection interviewing skills are an important part of the skills portfolio that people professionals need to possess. They are dealt with in this chapter under the following headings:

1 The selection interview: purpose and nature

2 Preparing for the interview

3 Conducting the selection interview

4 Coming to a conclusion

5 Tips

The selection interview: purpose and nature

The purpose of a selection interview is to obtain the information required to predict the extent to which the applicant will be able to carry out a job successfully.

Interviews can be conducted face-to-face or, more frequently nowadays, by telephone or video, and they can be structured or unstructured. But these different kinds of selection interviews have one characteristic in common – they are conversations with a purpose. They are conversations because candidates should be given the opportunity to talk freely about their careers and experience. And this conversation has to be planned, directed and controlled by the interviewer.

Methods of conducting selection interviews

Face-to-face interviews

Face-to-face interviews are the traditional method used in a selection process. They simply get candidates to answer questions designed to establish if they have the right knowledge, skills and abilities for the job. The face-to-face interview provides a better opportunity than other methods for interviewers to make an assessment (a subjective judgement) of the extent to which the candidates will 'fit' in with their boss, their colleagues and the culture of the organization.

Telephone interviews

Telephone interviews speed up the recruitment process. They are used to screen applicants and enable interviewers to decide which ones they would like to take further. But they have to be planned and conducted carefully because of the limitations imposed by the lack of face-to-face contact. However, interviewers are unable to judge things like personal appearance, body language, and to some extent personality, on the telephone.

Telephone interviews should be used simply to confirm or amplify basic information about candidates – whether they have the required skills and experience, can communicate in a clear way, can explain anything you're unsure about on their CV and, afterwards, whether or not more should be found out about them by seeing them in person. Planning for a telephone interview means reading the candidate's CV carefully to assess the extent to which it meets the person specification for the job. A set of questions should be prepared which would be put to each candidate.

The interview should be kept succinct; no rambling on the part of either the candidate or the interviewer. It should not last longer than 20 or 30 minutes. Make and keep notes in case a decision not to proceed is challenged.

If the phone interview goes well, a face-to-face interview with the candidate can be arranged. If the interview did not go well, tell the person at that time that their qualifications did not appear to meet what the company is currently looking for but thank them for their interest.

Video interviews

Like telephone interviews, video interviews can reduce the length of an interview programme. They have the obvious advantage over telephone interviews that there is visual as well as aural contact between the two parties. However, care has to be taken in making judgements in the somewhat artificial context of a videoed conversation. And, as in the case of telephone interviews, careful preparation is necessary. A decision to offer a job can be made entirely on the basis of a video interview although a face-to-face follow-up interview is better in most circumstances.

Structured interviews

The most important skill required in selection interviewing is conducting a structured interview. This is one based on predetermined questions put to all the candidates so that they can be compared against the same criteria. They are sometimes called competency-based interviews because they focus on the competencies required to do the job. A scoring system can be developed for comparative purposes. Research by Schmidt and Hunter (1998) showed that such interviews are much more likely to provide an accurate prediction of how someone will perform in a role than an unstructured interview. The three main types of structured interview are competency-based, strength-based and values-based. Of these, competency-based interviews are by far the most popular.

Competency-based interviews

A competency-based interview is a structured interview in which the questions put to all candidates aim to establish the extent to which they have the competencies required to perform the job as set out in the person specification. The interview will focus on what are sometimes called 'technical competencies' (the knowledge, skills and abilities required). But it will also cover 'behavioural competencies' – the types of behaviour required for successful performance of a role, for example communication, leadership and teamwork.

Strength-based interviews

A strengths-based interview is a structured interview in which the focus is on finding out the strengths of candidates – what they are good at doing. It involves asking questions such as 'What are you good at?' 'What comes easily to you?' and 'What have you done recently that you are proud of?' It is often used with graduates and school leavers who have little work experience. The strengths that are important in a job can be established by identifying the strengths of existing high performers in a similar job.

Values-based interviews

A values-based interview is a form of structured interview that aims to establish the extent to which the values of the candidate are in line with those of the organization.

Unstructured interviews

Unstructured interviews take the form of a general discussion during which the interviewer asks a few questions that are relevant to what he or she is looking for but without any specific aim in mind other than getting an overall picture of the candidate's suitability for a job. They are typically used by unskilled or untrained interviewers. Extensive research has shown that unstructured interviews are not very effective. Structured interviews are much better.

Preparing for the interview

It is necessary to prepare for the interview by carrying out the following steps.

Step 1. Know what you are looking for

In the first place you need to understand what you are looking for in terms of the knowledge, skills and abilities (KSAs) required to do the job. Consideration should also be given to the types and levels of education, training and experience, and the competencies (behavioural characteristics) that are likely to result in an acceptable level of KSAs. This information can be recorded in a person specification and will provide the basis upon which the questions to be put to candidates can be prepared.

Step 2. Review information about candidates

You should then consider the information candidates provide for themselves in, for example, their CVs, application forms, emails, letters or during a preliminary telephone or videoed conversation. This will identify any special questions you should ask about their career or to fill in any gaps, for example: 'You left your job in C and started in D. Would you mind telling me what you were doing during this time?'

Step 3 Plan the interview

A selection interview consists of three parts: (1) the opening, where the candidate is welcomed and put at ease, (2) the middle, in which a pre-planned sequence of questions is put to the candidate and (3) the end, in which the candidate can ask questions and is informed about the next steps, e.g. that if a provisional offer is accepted, references will be taken up with the candidate's existing employer.

You should decide at this stage how long you want to spend on each interview. As a rule of thumb, 45 to 60 minutes is usually required for senior professional or technical appointments. Middle-ranking jobs need about 30 to 45 minutes. The more routine jobs can be covered in 20 to 30 minutes. But the time allowed depends on the job and you do not want to insult a candidate by conducting a superficial interview.

You need to give some thought to how you are going to sequence the middle, information-seeking, part of an interview. The most popular approach is the chronological biographical interview which starts with the first job, or even before that at school and, if appropriate, college or university. The succeeding jobs, if any, are then dealt with in turn ending with the present job on which most time is spent. If you are not careful, however, using the chronological method for someone who has had a number of jobs can mean spending too much time on the earlier jobs, leaving insufficient time for the most important recent experiences. To overcome this problem, an alternative biographical approach is to start with the present job, which is discussed in some depth. The interviewer then works backwards, job by job, but only concentrating on particularly interesting or relevant experience in earlier jobs.

The problem with the biographical approach is that you can miss an important piece of information about the candidate. This is because there is a risk of concentrating on a succession of jobs and what, broadly, they entail rather than focusing on those aspects of a candidate's experience that illustrate their ability to carry out the role for which they are being considered.

This risk can be avoided by conducting a structured or targeted interview which is based on an analysis of the person specification in order to identify the criteria you will use to judge the suitability of the candidate. You 'target' these key criteria during the interview by asking appropriate questions about the experience, knowledge, skills, capabilities, values and personal qualities of candidates, the answers to which can then be compared with the criteria to assess the extent to which candidates meet the specification.

Conducting the selection interview

The skills needed to conduct an effective selection interview are establishing rapport, questioning, listening and keeping control.

Establishing rapport

Establishing rapport means creating a good relationship with candidates – getting on their wavelength, putting them at ease, encouraging them to respond and generally being friendly. This is not just a question of being 'nice' to them. If you achieve rapport you are more likely to get them to talk freely about both their strengths and weaknesses.

Good rapport is created by the way in which you greet candidates, how you start the interview and how you put your questions and respond to replies. Questions should not be posed aggressively or imply that you are criticizing some aspect of the candidate's career. Some people like the idea of 'stress' interviews but they are counterproductive. Candidates clam up and gain a negative impression of you and the organization.

When responding to answers you should be appreciative, not critical: 'Thank you, that was very helpful; now can we go on to...' – not, 'Well, it seems to me that things did not go according to plan.'

Body language can also be important. If you maintain natural eye contact, avoid slumping in your seat, nod and make encouraging comments when appropriate, you will establish better rapport and get more out of the interview.

Questioning

Questioning is the key skill interviewers need to possess. Questions draw candidates out and elicit the information the interviewer has decided should be obtained to reach a conclusion. To this end it is desirable to ask open-ended questions – questions that cannot be answered by 'yes' or 'no' and which promote a full response. Biased questions referring to gender, race, sexual orientation, disability or age must be avoided, as advised by Moore (2017):

> Each interview question should have a point. It ought to be able to assess some work-relevant ability or behaviour. As such, it should be easy for interviewers to specify beforehand what a good answer might look like.

The following are 10 useful questions from which you can select any that are relevant:

1 What are the most important aspects of your present job?

2 What do you think have been your most notable achievements in your career to date?

3 What sort of problems have you successfully solved recently in your job?

4 What have you learned from your present job?

5 What has been your experience in...?

6 What do you know about...?

7 What is your approach to handling...?

8 What particularly interests you in this job and why?

9 Which aspects of your experience do you think are most relevant for this job?

10 Is there anything else relating to your career that hasn't come out yet in this interview, but you think I ought to hear about?

These questions might be extended by what are called work sample tests that give an indication of how well the candidate would perform important parts of the job. You can also consider the use of strength-based or value-based questions, examples of which are given below.

Strength-based interview questions

Strength-based questions focus on what people are good at. They are particularly suitable when interviewing graduates, school leavers or students who have had little relevant work experience.

- What are you good at doing?
- What comes easily to you?
- What do you learn quickly?
- What did you find easiest to learn at school or university?
- What subjects did you most enjoy studying?
- What things give you energy?
- Describe a successful day you have had.
- When did you achieve something you were really proud of?

Value-based interview questions

The aim of value-based questions such as the following is to establish the values of candidates about different aspects of work and to assess how compatible they are with those of the organization:

- Have you ever faced an ethical dilemma at work? If so, what was the issue and what did you do?

- What company policies would you suggest creating to make their operations more environmentally friendly? How would you ensure employees understand and apply these guidelines?

- Why is good teamwork important and how can it be achieved?

- Are there any situations in which you think the needs of the individual are more important than the needs of the organization?

- What do you think a line manager should do if a member of her or his team is suspected of bullying a fellow worker?

- Do you think organizations should be concerned with the financial wellbeing of their employees and if so, why?

Listening

A selection interview can be described as a conversation with a purpose and listening skills are important. You need to:

- Concentrate on what the candidate is saying, following not only words but also body language, which often underlines meaning and gives life to the message.

- Respond quickly to points made by the candidate, if only in the shape of encouraging grunts.

- Ask questions frequently to elucidate meaning and to give the candidate an opportunity to rephrase or underline a point.

- Comment on the points made by the candidate, without interrupting the flow, in order to test understanding and demonstrate that the speaker and listener are still on the same wavelength. These comments may reflect back or summarize something the candidate has said, thus giving an opportunity for her or him to reconsider or elucidate the point made.

- Make notes on the key points – even if the notes are not referred to later, they will help to concentrate the mind.

- Continuously evaluate the messages being delivered to check that they are understood and relevant to the purpose of the interview.

- Be alert at all times to the nuances of what the candidate is saying.

- Let the candidate go on with the minimum of interruption.

Keeping control

You want candidates to talk, but not too much. When preparing for the interview you should have drawn up an agenda and you must try to stick to it. Don't cut candidates short too brutally but say something like: 'Thank you, I've got a good picture of that, now what about...?'

Focus on specifics as much as you can. If candidates ramble on a bit or their replies to your questions lack substance, ask a pointed question (a 'probe' question) that asks for an example illustrating the particular aspect of their work that you are considering.

Common interviewing mistakes

A skilled interviewer avoids the following common mistakes:

- coming to firm conclusions on inadequate evidence and making snap or hurried judgements – many interviewers make up their minds about a candidate within a few minutes of meeting them on the basis of their appearance, manner or speech and before asking any questions;
- jumping to conclusions on a single piece of favourable evidence – the 'halo effect';
- jumping to conclusions on a single piece of unfavourable evidence – the 'horns effect';
- not weighing up the balance between the favourable and unfavourable evidence logically and objectively;
- failing to ensure that candidates support what they say about what they have done or can do with examples from their personal experience;
- making biased judgements on the grounds of sex, race, age, disability, religion, appearance, accent, class or any aspect of the candidate's life history, circumstances or career which do not fit the preconceptions of what you are looking for.

Coming to a conclusion

Candidates can be assessed on the basis of the answers they have given to structured questions. The answers could be scored on a scale of, say, 1 to 10. These assessments can inform an overall assessment of knowledge, skills and abilities. Any clearly unsuitable candidate could be rejected at this initial stage.

Next, compare the assessment of each of the remaining potentially successful candidates against one another to reach a conclusion on the preferred candidate. You can then reach a conclusion on those preferred by reference to their assessments under each heading.

In the end, the decision between qualified candidates could well be judgemental. There may be one suitable candidate but there could be two or three (although sometimes there may be none at all). Where there is a choice, a balanced view has to be reached by reference to interview notes and ratings. Don't, however, settle for second best in desperation. It is better to try again.

A record of the reasons for the choice and why candidates have been rejected should be kept for at least six months in case the decision is challenged as being discriminatory. An example of an interview rating form is given in Table 8.1.

Table 8.1   Example of an interview rating form

Questions	Assessment of answers				Comments
	Unacceptable 1–2	Marginally acceptable 3–4	Acceptable 5–8	Very acceptable 9–10	
Overall suitability					

TIPS

Table 8.2   Selection interviewing tips

Do	Don't
• Plan the interview. • Give yourself sufficient time. • Use a structured interview approach involving the use of predetermined questions put to all the candidates for a job. • Create the right atmosphere. • Establish an easy and informal relationship – start with an undemanding question. • Encourage the candidate to talk. • Cover the ground as planned, ensuring that you complete a prepared agenda and maintain continuity. • Analyse the candidate's career to reveal strengths, weaknesses and patterns of interest. • Make use of open questions which invite people to talk. • Ensure that questions are clear and unambiguous. • Get examples and instances of the successful application of knowledge, skills and the effective use of capabilities. • Make judgements on the basis of the factual information you have obtained about candidates' experience and attributes in relation to the person specification. • Keep control over the content and timing of the interview.	• Start the interview unprepared. • Plunge too quickly into demanding questions. • Ask multiple or leading questions. • Pay too much attention to isolated strengths or weaknesses. • Allow candidates to gloss over important facts. • Talk too much or allow candidates to ramble on. • Allow your prejudices to get the better of your capacity to make objective judgements. • Fall into the halo effect trap – i.e. drawing conclusions about a person on the basis of one or two good points, leading to the neglect of negative indicators – or into the horns trap, focusing too much on one or two weak points. • Ask questions or make remarks that could be construed as in any way discriminatory. • Attempt too many interviews in a row.

References

Moore, D A (2017) How to improve the accuracy and reduce the cost of personnel selection, *California Management Review*, **60** (1), pp 8–17

Schmidt, F L and Hunter, J E (1998) The validity and utility of selection methods in personnel psychology: practical and theoretical implications of 85 years of research findings, *Psychological Bulletin*, **124** (2), pp 262–74

Learning and development skills

09

HR professionals are often responsible for enhancing the knowledge and skills of employees and for providing guidance to line managers on conducting their learning and development (L&D) activities. They therefore need to know about the following:

1 Developing L&D strategy

2 Coaching

3 Mentoring

4 Facilitating

5 Job instruction

6 Tips

Developing L&D strategy

Learning and development strategy sets out what an organization intends to do about developing the capabilities of employees through its learning policies and practices. When formulating L&D strategy the aim is to develop an understanding shared by all stakeholders of the direction it is believed learning and development should go. Proposals should be relevant, realistic and actionable. They should respond to but also anticipate the critical needs of the organization and the people in it. They should be evidence-based – founded on detailed analysis and study, not just wishful thinking – and should incorporate the experienced and collective judgement of top management about organizational requirements while also taking into account the views of line managers and employees generally. L&D strategies should be tailored to reflect the needs of the future rather than mirroring current conditions or past practices. They may fundamentally be business-led but it can be a reciprocal process – an analysis of the needs of the business for skills or a review of the issues facing the business in obtaining those skills can lead to the identification of problems in implementing the business strategy that needs to be addressed.

Coaching

Coaching is a personal (usually one-to-one) approach that enables people to develop their skills and knowledge and improve their performance. As Whitmore (2002) suggested: 'Coaching is unlocking a person's potential to maximize their own performance. It is helping them to learn rather than teaching them.' Clutterbuck (2004) noted: 'Coaching is primarily focused on performance within the current job and emphasizes the development of skills.'

Coaching is often provided by specialists from inside or outside the organization who concentrate on specific areas of skills or behaviour, for example leadership. But it is also something that people professionals have to be prepared to do as part of their normal learning and development duties, and this means deploying the skills described below.

The approach to coaching

To succeed in coaching you need to understand that your role is to help people to learn and ensure that they are motivated to learn. They should be aware of the advantages to them as well as the organization of developing their present level of knowledge or skill or modifying their behaviour. Individuals should be given guidance on what they should be learning and feedback on how well they are doing and, because learning is an active and not a passive process, they should be actively involved with their coach.

Coaching is sometimes informal, but it has to be planned. It is not simply checking from time to time on what people are doing and then advising them on how to do it better. Nor is it occasionally telling people where they have gone wrong and throwing in a lecture for good measure. As far as possible, coaching should take place within the framework of a general plan of the areas and direction in which individuals will benefit from further development. Coaching plans should be incorporated into the personal development plans set out in a performance agreement.

Coaching should provide motivation, structure and effective feedback. As a coach, you should believe that people can succeed and that they can contribute to their own success.

Coaching styles

Clutterbuck and Megginson (2005) identified four coaching styles:

1 *Assessor* – this is akin to instruction and involves telling people the way to do something.

2 *Demonstrator* – this is less directive than the assessor style. It involves showing learners how to do something and then getting them to do it with guidance and comments from the coach as required.

3 *Tutor* – this involves encouraging learners to find out how to do things for themselves. It is still relatively directive as it is the coach who suggests what learners should look for.

4 *Stimulator* – this helps learners to teach themselves by guiding their thinking through the use of insight-provoking questions.

Criteria for effectiveness

The following criteria for evaluating the performance of a coach were listed by Gray (2010):

- establishes rapport;
- creates trust and respect;
- demonstrates effective communication skills;
- promotes self-awareness and self-knowledge;
- uses active listening and questioning techniques;
- assists goal development and setting;
- motivates;
- encourages alternative perspectives;
- assists in making sense of a situation;
- identifies significant patterns of thinking and behaving;
- provides an appropriate mix of challenge and support;
- facilitates depth of understanding;

- shows compassion;
- acts ethically;
- inspires curiosity;
- acts as a role model;
- values diversity and difference;
- promotes action and reflection.

Mentoring

Mentors offer guidance, pragmatic advice and continuing support to help those allocated to them to learn and develop. It is a method of helping people to learn as distinct from coaching, which can be a relatively directive means of increasing people's competence. Mentors may be line managers. They are often appointed and given training by people management or L&D specialists who therefore need to be aware of the skills required. People and L&D professionals may act as mentors themselves, although experienced managers are best if they have the skills and enthusiasm required.

Mentors provide people with:

- advice in drawing up self-development programmes or learning contracts;
- general help with learning programmes;
- guidance on how to acquire the necessary knowledge and skills to do a new job;
- advice on dealing with any administrative, technical or people problems individuals meet, especially in the early stages of their careers;
- information on 'the way things are done around here' – the corporate culture in terms of expected behaviour;
- coaching in specific skills;
- help in tackling projects – not by doing it for them but by pointing them in the right direction, helping people to help themselves;
- a parental figure with whom individuals can discuss their aspirations and concerns and who will lend a sympathetic ear to their problems.

Mentors need to adopt a non-directive but supportive approach to helping the person or persons they are dealing with.

Facilitating

The facilitation of learning is the process of helping people to learn mainly for themselves rather than force-feeding them. The aim of the facilitator is to guide thinking rather than simply imparting new knowledge. Facilitating may simply be the process of ensuring that employees and individuals have the opportunity to develop their skills and abilities. But, as described below, it is also an important technique for use in learning groups for formal or semi-formal training interventions.

The facilitator of a learning group has to unobtrusively stimulate group members to talk, move the discussion along predetermined lines (there must be a plan and an ultimate objective), and provide interim summaries and a final summary. Help in reaching conclusions is provided by asking questions that encourage people to think for themselves. These can be challenging and probing questions, but the facilitator does not provide the answers – that is the role of the people involved. Neither do facilitators allow their own opinions to intrude – they are there to help people to learn, not to enforce their own ideas.

Job instruction

When people learn specific tasks, especially those involving basic administrative or manual skills, the learning will be more effective if job instruction techniques are used. People professionals may possibly be involved in providing direct instruction, but their most typical role is that of promoting effective instruction techniques for use by line managers and others involved in workplace learning or running formal training programmes. They should therefore be aware of the sequence of instruction, as described below.

Preparation

Preparation for each instruction period means that the trainer must have a plan for presenting the subject matter and using appropriate teaching methods, visual aids and demonstration aids. It also means preparing trainees for the instruction that is to follow. They should want to learn. They must perceive that the learning will be relevant and useful to them personally.

They should be encouraged to take pride in their job and to appreciate the satisfaction that comes from skilled performance.

Presentation

Presentation should consist of a combination of telling and showing – explanation and demonstration. Explanation should be as simple and direct as possible: the trainer briefly explains the ground to be covered and what to look for. He or she makes the maximum use of charts, diagrams and other visual aids. The aim should be to teach first things first and then proceed from the known to the unknown, the simple to the complex, the concrete to the abstract, the general to the particular, the observation to reasoning, and the whole to the parts and back to the whole again.

Demonstration

Demonstration is an essential stage in instruction, especially when the skill to be learnt is mainly a 'doing' skill. Demonstration can take place in three stages:

1 The complete operation is shown at normal speed to show the trainee how the task should be carried out eventually.

2 The operation is demonstrated slowly and in correct sequence, element by element, to indicate clearly what is done and the order in which each task is carried out.

3 The operation is demonstrated again slowly, at least two or three times, to stress the how, when and why of successive movements.

The learner then practises by imitating the instructor and constantly repeating the operation under guidance. The aim is to reach the target level of performance for each element of the total task, but the instructor must constantly strive to develop coordinated and integrated performance – that is, the smooth combination of the separate elements of the task into a whole job pattern.

Follow-up

Follow-up continues during the training period for all the time required by the learner to reach a level of performance equal to that of the normal experienced worker in terms of quality, speed and attention to safety. During the follow-up stage, the learner will continue to need help with particularly difficult tasks or to overcome temporary setbacks that result in a deterioration of performance. The instructor may have to repeat the presentation for the elements and supervise practice more closely until the trainee regains confidence or masters the task.

TIPS

- Work with leaders to define and communicate a vision for learning clearly linked to organizational objectives.
- Consider whether there are appropriate policies and processes in place to promote individual and team learning.
- Encourage line managers to be fully involved in improving the quality of learning in their departments, advise them on how to set about it and provide coaching as required on how to do so.
- Promote self-directed learning, which involves individuals taking charge of the whole learning process. Provide them with guidance and help in doing so.
- Facilitate 'learning in the flow of work' – workplace learning.
- Develop coaching, mentoring, facilitating and instruction skills.

References

Clutterbuck, D (2004) *Everyone Needs a Mentor: Fostering talent in your organization*, 4th edition, London, CIPD

Clutterbuck, D and Megginson, D (2005) *Making Coaching Work: Creating a coaching culture*, London, CIPD

Gray, D A (2010) Building quality into executive coaching, in (eds) J Gold, R Thorpe and A Mumford, *Gower Handbook of Leadership and Management Development*, Farnham, Gower, pp 367–85

Whitmore, J (2002) *Coaching for Performance*, 3rd edition, London, Nicholas Brealey

Reward management skills

10

People management professionals are concerned with the development and operation of reward systems. What this involves is examined in this chapter under the following headings:

1 The nature of reward management

2 Reward management responsibilities

3 Reward management skills

4 Tips

The nature of reward management

Reward management is the development and implementation of reward processes, practices and procedures covering how:

- base pay is determined through job evaluation and market pricing and managed through formal pay structures or informally;
- performance and skill are valued and rewarded through base pay progression and/or bonuses (the latter are sometimes called 'variable pay');
- employee benefits such as pensions and wellbeing programmes are provided.

Reward management responsibilities

People professionals:

- develop and implement reward strategies that support the achievement of corporate strategy and ensure that the contribution of employees is valued;

- formulate and advise on reward policies on levels of reward, the relative emphasis that should be given to achieving internal equity and external competitiveness, and the degree of transparency that should exist on how the reward system operates;
- advise line managers on exercising their responsibilities for reward;
- develop and apply methods to establish equitable pay levels (job evaluation) and the rates of pay needed to keep rewards competitive (market pricing);
- design and maintain pay structures that facilitate the management of reward;
- advise on the methods that should be used to achieve pay progression, for example pay-for-performance schemes;
- advise on the use of one-off bonus payments to reward achievement and contribution, including in some cases the design and administration of executive bonus schemes;
- advise remuneration committees on executive pay matters including the use of external consultants,
- develop and administer employee benefits packages including the use of flexible benefits;
- provide for the financial wellbeing of employees;
- review data on the levels and distribution of pay (reward analytics) and initiate action to deal with anomalies and inequity;
- prepare and submit the required statutory reports on pay;
- administer reward arrangements including pay reviews and the payroll.

Reward management skills

To carry out their reward management duties people professionals need analytical skills and to be numerate, creative and good communicators. They also need to:

- understand the business strategy and how reward management policy and practice will contribute to the achievement of that strategy;
- be aware of the organization's core competencies – what it is good at doing;

- know how performance in the organization is measured in financial and non-financial terms;

- tailor reward policies and practices to suit the particular goals, character and culture of the organization;

- keep up with leading-edge approaches to reward management;

- apply administrative expertise to deliver efficient and well-serviced reward processes.

TIPS

- Recognize the right of employees to be rewarded fairly for the work they do and align reward policies accordingly.

- Help to shift the organization's culture to become more performance-oriented.

- Take active steps to understand the business or corporate strategy and develop reward policies and practices that support the achievement of organizational goals.

- Develop a mix of generalist and specialist knowledge and expertise, always bearing in mind the strategic direction and needs of the organization and the character and needs of employees and line managers.

- Establish a balanced and productive partnership relationship with line managers. Balance devolving responsibility for operating reward processes to them with the need to ensure that reward policy guidelines are followed and reward decisions are fair and consistent.

- Practice an open, transparent and engaging approach to reward management. Involve line managers and employees directly and as early as possible in diagnosing your current reward need and priorities, and especially regarding any changes and improvements you are considering. Ideally have regular forums to gauge their needs, views and reactions.

- Train newly appointed managers (and retrain existing managers as necessary) in their reward management responsibilities. Provide guidance and help from reward specialists whenever it is needed, and in person if required, not just in intranet policies and guidelines.

- Establish clear criteria for the performance and success of your reward function and the reward policies and practices it develops and advises on. Monitor, regularly report on and evaluate reward policies and decisions, and advise senior leaders and line managers on alternative approaches and improvements as necessary.

- Use external reward consultants as necessary to supplement and extend in-house expertise and experience. Use these experiences to build and apply process and change management skills in the function, which appear to be particularly important in ensuring the successful implementation and effective operation and employee experience of reward policies.

PART THREE
Analytical, technical and research skills

Analytical and diagnostic skills 11

The effectiveness of people management initiatives and decisions depends largely on the use of analytical and diagnostic skills as described in this chapter under the following headings:

1 Analytical skills

2 Diagnostic skills

3 Tips

Analytical skills

Analysis is the process of subjecting a complex situation or problem to a detailed and thorough examination in order to understand its essential features and explain the causes of events. This understanding is enhanced by breaking the situation down into its constituent parts.

The application of analytical skills enables people to dig into problems and come out with facts-based solutions by providing the basis for a diagnosis of the cause or causes of a problem and the considerations that will affect any decision. Analytical skills are needed to gain insight into people management issues and the factors that should be taken into account when developing people management policy and practice. In accordance with attribution theory, the validity of such explanations depends on:

- the degree of distinctiveness – the extent to which the event and its consequences are observable;

- consistency – the extent to which the event and its effect remains the same over time; and

- consensus – the degree of agreement among the views of individuals of the relationship between the event and its impact.

Analytical skills involve the ability to understand the big picture but also the capacity to deconstruct information into smaller categories in order to draw conclusions and find patterns and trends. They are used to break down overall impressions in order to reach a better understanding of what is going on. This is done by isolating the factors involved to establish their relative significance.

Diagnostic tools such as engagement surveys can be used to support analysis.

Diagnostic skills

Diagnostic skills are used to identify and define any HR issues or problems in the whole organization or part of it in order to resolve them. A diagnosis is based on the evidence assembled by an analysis of what is happening and predictions of what might happen if nothing is done about it.

The diagnosis starts with a look at the whole picture to gain an overall view of the situation, issue or problem. The next step is to penetrate beneath the surface impression. Critical thinking and logical reasoning are used to ensure that explanations are valid and to support conclusions (see Chapter 12). Questions have to be answered:

- 'What's actually going on here?'
- 'What are the real issues?'
- 'What's involved?'
- 'Who's involved?'
- 'What are the factors affecting these issues?'
- 'What are the characteristics of each of those factors?'
- 'What is the relative significance of them given the situation we are in?'
- 'To what extent do we have to deal with these factors separately?'
- 'Where do we go from here?'

The diagnostic skills required to do this comprise the ability to use critical reasoning skills, first to establish from evidence the significant features of a situation, second to understand the nature and cause of that situation, and third to draw conclusions on what needs to be done on the basis of that evidence and understanding. The aim is to ensure that explanations are valid and to support conclusions so that an appropriate way forward can be selected.

TIPS

- Base problem solving and decision making on thorough analysis.

- Use analytical skills to establish the facts and obtain other relevant evidence.

- Use diagnostic skills to understand, articulate and deal with issues and problems.

Critical thinking skills 12

Critical thinking involves reflecting on and interpreting data, using logical reasoning to draw warranted conclusions and recognize ill-defined assumptions. It is an important feature of analysis, as discussed in Chapter 11, but people professionals need the ability to use it whenever they have to evaluate what they are proposing or doing and to assess what other people propose or suggest. This chapter is set out under the following headings:

1 The need for critical skills

2 Critical thinking

3 Critical evaluation

4 Developing and justifying arguments

5 Tips

The need for critical skills

Critical skills are needed to provide for clear and logical thinking – a necessary skill for people professionals who are constantly faced with problems to be solved and decisions to be made. The following are words of wisdom from the philosopher L Susan Stebbing (1939):

> One of the greatest difficulties at the outset of the attempt to think effectively consists in the difficulty of recognizing what we know as distinguished from what we do not know but merely take for granted. Further, it is not always easy to distinguish between what we may reasonably believe and what we ought to hold as doubtful and in need of confirmation. It is reasonable to accept a statement as true, ie to hold a belief, provided that there is some evidence in support of it and that this does not contradict what we already know to be the case. Perhaps few people would deny that we all hold beliefs which are not in this sense reasonable.

Critical thinking

Critical thinking is the process of analysing and evaluating the quality of ideas, theories and concepts to establish the degree to which they are valid and supported by the evidence and the extent to which they are biased.

'Critical' in this context does not mean disapproval or being negative. There are many positive uses of critical thinking, for example testing a hypothesis, proving a proposition or evaluating a concept, theory or argument. Critical thinking can occur whenever people weigh up evidence and make a judgement, solve a problem or reach a decision. The aim is to come to well-reasoned conclusions and solutions and to test them against relevant criteria and standards. Critical thinking calls for the ability to:

- recognize problems and establish ways of dealing with them;
- gather and marshal pertinent (relevant) information;
- identify unstated assumptions and values;
- interpret data, to appraise evidence and to evaluate arguments;
- recognize the existence (or non-existence) of logical relationships between propositions;
- draw warranted conclusions and make valid generalizations;
- test assertions, conclusions and generalizations;
- reconstruct ideas or beliefs by examining and analysing relevant evidence.

Critical evaluation

Critical evaluation is the process of making informed judgements about the validity, relevance and usefulness of ideas and arguments. It means not taking anything for granted and, where necessary, challenging propositions. It uses critical thinking by analysing and evaluating the quality of theories and concepts to establish the degree to which they are valid and supported by the evidence (evidence-based) and the extent to which they are biased. The arguments for and against are weighed and the strength of the evidence on both sides is assessed. On the basis of this assessment, a conclusion is reached on which proposition or argument is to be preferred. Critical evaluation is required when testing research-based propositions.

Testing research-based propositions

Propositions based on research investigations and evidence can be tested by using the following checklist:

- Was the scope of the investigation sufficiently comprehensive?

- Was the research methodology sufficiently rigorous and appropriate?

- Are the instances representative or are they selected simply to support a point of view?

- Are there contradictory instances that have not been looked for?

- Does the proposition conflict with other propositions for which there are equally good grounds?

- If there are any conflicting beliefs or contradictory items of evidence, have they been put to the test against the original proposition?

- Could the evidence lead to other equally valid conclusions?

- Are there any other factors that have not been taken into account that may have influenced the evidence and, therefore, the conclusion?

Critical evaluation does not necessarily mean negative criticism; it means reaching a judgement based on analysis and evidence, and the judgement can be positive as well as negative.

Logical reasoning

If you say people are logical, you mean that they draw reasonable inferences – their conclusions can be proved by reference to the facts used to support them – and they avoid ill-founded and tendentious arguments, generalizations and irrelevancies. Logical reasoning is the basis of critical thinking and evaluation. It takes place when there is a clear relationship (a line of reasoning) between the premise (the original proposition) and the conclusion, which is supported by valid and reliable evidence and does not rely on fallacious or misleading argument. Logical reasoning is what L Susan Stebbing (1939) called 'Thinking to some purpose'. Clear thinking is required to establish the validity of a proposition, concept or idea.

It is necessary to question assumptions, especially when a belief is expressed as a fact. You need to ask yourself – and others – 'What's the evidence for that?' You have to spot fallacious and misleading arguments. A fallacy is an unsound form of argument leading to an error in reasoning or a misleading impression. The most common forms of fallacies that need to be discerned in other people's arguments or avoided in one's own are summarized below:

- *Affirming the consequent* – leaping to the conclusion that a hypothesis is true because a single cause of the consequence has been observed.

- *Begging the question* – taking for granted what has yet to be proved.

- *Chop logic* – 'Contrarywise', said Tweedledee, 'if it was so, it might be, and if it were so, it would be; but as it isn't it ain't. That's logic.' Chop logic may not always be as bad as that, but it is about drawing false conclusions and using dubious methods of argument. For example: selecting instances favourable to a contention while ignoring those that are counter to it; twisting an argument used by an opponent to mean something quite different from what was intended; diverting opponents by throwing on them the burden of proof for something they have not maintained; ignoring the point in dispute, changing the question to one that is less awkward to answer; and reiterating what has been denied and ignoring what has been asserted. Politicians know all about chop logic.

- *Confusing correlation with causation* – assuming that because A is associated with B it has caused B. It may or may not have.

- *False antithesis* – the error of thinking two things are in opposition to one another when really they are not.

- *False choice* – a situation in which only two alternatives are considered, when in fact there are additional options.

- *Potted thinking* – using slogans and catchphrases to extend an assertion in an unwarrantable fashion.

- *Reaching false conclusions* – forming the view that because some are, then all are. An assertion about several cases is twisted into an assertion about all cases. The conclusion does not follow the premise. This is what logicians call the 'undistributed middle'.

- *Selective reasoning* – selecting instances favourable to a contention while ignoring those that conflict with it.

- *Sweeping statements* – over-simplifying the facts.

- *Special pleading* – focusing too much on one's own case and failing to see that there may be other points of view.

Developing and justifying arguments

An argument as an aspect of critical thinking consists of a presentation of reasons that support a contention. It consists of:

- a proposition or statement that expresses a point of view or belief;
- the reasoning that makes a case for the proposition or point of view;
- a discussion, the aim of which is to get the reader or listener to agree with the case that has been made;
- a conclusion that sums up the argument and its significance.

Developing an argument

An argument is based (predicated) on a premise (the proposition) that sets out the underpinning assumption. There may be more than one proposition or assumption. It could be phrased something like this: 'The argument is that A is the case. It is predicated on the assumption that B and C apply.' In a sense this suggests what conclusion the argument is intended to reach but it also indicates that this conclusion depends on the validity of the assumptions, which will have to be proved (there are such things as false premises).

Justifying an argument

The argument continues by supplying reasons to accept the proposition or point of view. These reasons have to be supported by evidence, which should be based on valid research, rigorous observation, or relevant and verifiable experience, not on hearsay. It involves logical reasoning, which avoids the fallacies referred to earlier and requires critical thinking, which involves coming to well-reasoned conclusions and solutions and testing them against relevant criteria and standards. It also demands critical evaluation, which means reflecting on and interpreting data, drawing warranted conclusions and identifying faulty reasoning, dubious assumptions and biases.

TIPS

- Use critical thinking and critical evaluation techniques to analyse and evaluate the quality of ideas, theories and concepts in order to establish the degree to which they are valid and supported by the evidence and assess the extent to which they are biased.

- Base problem solving and decision making on critical thinking and logical reasoning.
- Always question assumptions, especially when a belief is expressed as a fact.
- Never take anything for granted and always challenge doubtful propositions.

Reference

Stebbing, L Susan (1939) *Thinking to Some Purpose*, Harmondsworth, Penguin Books

Evidence-based people management skills 13

Evidence-based management is the process of ensuring that conclusions are reached and decisions are made by means of the critical evaluation of the evidence from multiple sources. The CIPD's Profession Map (2022) states that 'professional judgement should be driven by the best available evidence'. It is covered in this chapter under the following headings:

1 Evidence-based people management defined

2 The process of evidence-based people management

3 Tips

Evidence-based people management defined

Evidence-based people management bases decisions about people strategies, innovations and practices on the information obtained from the analysis and evaluation of data provided by people analytics (see Chapter 14) and the information produced by benchmarking and research. The aim is to ensure that these decisions are based on factual evidence, not guesswork or supposition.

The process of evidence-based people management

Evidence-based people management starts by obtaining answers to one or the other of these questions:

1 'This is what we want to do; what evidence do we need to assemble to justify doing it?'

2 'This is the evidence; what conclusions can be drawn about what we should do about it?'

In the first case, the next step is to get the answer to the question: 'Where can this evidence be found?' The four sources of evidence for management decision making are: (1) organizational evidence collected by the use of people analytics, employee surveys and formal or informal discussions; (2) stakeholders' expectations; (3) benchmarking information on good people management practice elsewhere; and (4) published results of research. When evidence is obtained or already exists it is subjected to critical evaluation to establish the extent to which it is valid, relevant and supported by the facts. What appears to be valid evidence can simply be a matter of opinion and it is necessary to scrutinize facts and arguments carefully.

Decisions are reached by weighing up the evidence and answering the following questions:

- What does the evidence reveal about possible courses of action?
- Does the evidence support the case for a new or revised policy or practice?
- Does the evidence provide guidance on what is likely to be the best or at least the optimum course of action?

Evidence-based people management involves:

1 *Setting* people management goals and success criteria.

2 *Measuring* by getting the facts.

3 *Evaluating* the facts by subjecting them to critical evaluation.

4 *Developing* the strategy, policy or practice in the light of the evaluation and taking into account goals and success criteria.

5 *Implementing* the strategy, policy or practice.

6 *Reviewing* the effectiveness of the development by reference to the success criteria.

Figure 13.1 Inter-relationships between the components of evidence-based management

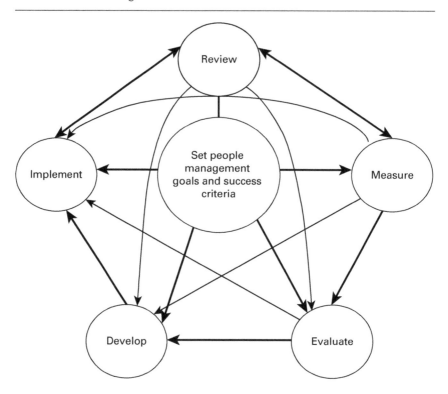

A model of how these activities are inter-related is shown in Figure 13.1.

The model illustrates how evidence-based people management can work. It represents a sequential progress in the form of a continuous cycle from goal setting, through review, measurement, evaluation and development activities to implementation and further review. This is the ideal approach but in reality the activities will not be necessarily specified, defined or managed in such an orderly sequence. They are closely interlinked and they may overlap. Goal setting affects all the other activities. Similarly, those concerned with review, measurement and evaluation can take place at any time (or all at once) and all of them directly influence the subsequent activities of development and implementation.

Using the components of the model appropriately means applying and linking them in ways that fit the demands of the situation. It becomes a way of thinking that people practitioners can apply to any situation or issue. Questions such as the following can be used to establish what the situation within the organization is, what needs to be done about it and what information is required to inform decisions:

- What are we trying to do here, what's important to this organization, how do we measure that?
- How are current practices helping or hindering what we are trying to do and what evidence do we have of this?
- How might changes improve the delivery of desired outcomes?
- How can we best implement improvements and how can we show ourselves that they are working?
- What evidence do we need to help us make the right decision on what to do?
- Where will that evidence come from and how will we obtain it?

TIPS

- Use a wide range of different kinds of evidence depending on the problem.
- Question ideas such as 'best practice'.
- Subject any evidence collected to critical evaluation (see Chapter 12).
- Replace conventional wisdom with a commitment to gather the necessary facts to make more intelligent and informed decisions.
- Check the basis of research evidence to ensure that it is valid (see Chapter 20).

Reference

Chartered Institute of Personnel and Development (2022) People Profession Map, London, CIPD, https://www.cipd.org/globalassets/media/comms/the-people-profession/profession-map-pdfs/profession-map_full-standards-download.pdf (archived at https://perma.cc/4PTS-WRHD)

People analytics 14
skills

People analytics applies measures or metrics (these terms are generally used interchangeably although strictly speaking, metrics are decimalized measures) to assess such things as employee turnover, levels of engagement and the impact of people management practices. This chapter is set out under the following headings:

1 The purpose of people analytics

2 The techniques of people analytics

3 Skills of people analytics

4 Tips

The purpose of people analytics

People analytics provides a basis for decision making. It assembles the information required for evidence-based management. The process of identifying appropriate measures and collecting and analysing data relating to them focuses attention on what needs to be done to find, keep, develop and make the best use of people and to treat them properly. Predictions can be made to provide guidance on the development of people strategy and progress can be monitored in achieving strategic goals. In accordance with the principle that 'you cannot manage what you cannot measure', the effectiveness and impact of people practices can be calculated.

In particular, people analytics help to:

- measure levels of engagement to assess progress in improving levels;
- analyse the incidence and reasons for employee turnover;
- investigate the extent and causes of absenteeism;
- assess the effectiveness of different sources of recruits;

- evaluate the impact of learning and development activities;
- review the effectiveness of performance management or performance-related pay in improving performance;
- measure the impact of organizational development interventions;
- investigate accident rates.

In each area the analysis would investigate trends and, whenever possible, the inter-relationships between different types of data and between the data and performance. This evidence could be used to reach conclusions about any action required or to evaluate the effectiveness of action already taken.

The techniques of people analytics

People analytics uses the 'triple-A' approach: Analysis-Assessment-Action. There are three types of analytics as described below.

Descriptive analytics

Descriptive analytics is the use of data to record a particular aspect of people management and provide information on what has been happening to, for example, labour turnover or absence rates. It covers the following types of data:

- Basic workforce data – demographic data (numbers by job category, sex, ethnicity, age, disability), working arrangements, absence and sickness, employee turnover, health and safety, pay.
- People development and performance data – learning and development programmes, performance management/potential assessments, skills and qualifications.
- Employee engagement data – engagement surveys.
- Perceptual data – opinion surveys, focus groups, exit interviews.
- Performance data – financial, operational and customer.

Multidimensional analytics

Multidimensional analytics is a form of descriptive analytics in which different sets of data or variables are compared to show the extent to which there is any relationship between them. It is concerned with independent and dependent variables. A variable is a factor or value that can change: an independent variable is one that is unaffected by other variables but can affect a dependent variable; a dependent variable is one that can be used to indicate how changes in the level of the independent variable relate to changes in the level of the dependent variable.

The analysis may show that the independent variable has a positive effect on the dependent variable. This is correlation. But this does not mean that it is the cause. However, even if causation cannot be established with confidence, the existence of correlation can be revealing. At least it can indicate that a positive relationship exists between a people management initiative and desirable outcomes. This can be used to justify the investment and point the way to further developments. It may be decided when making the hypothesis prior to the analysis that there are two or more independent variables that might affect the dependent variable. In this case multi-regression analysis is used (see Chapter 19).

Predictive analytics

Predictive people analytics involves the projection or prediction of a future situation on the basis of a study of present trends. By understanding as much as we possibly can about the past, it is possible to identify patterns and build models for what will happen in the future.

A predictive people analytics exercise makes use of multiple regression or multivariate analysis (see Chapter 19) to forecast the value of a dependent variable or variables based on the value of one or more independent variables. It can be used to predict such matters as employee engagement, employee turnover and levels of productivity or performance.

Skills required

The development and use of people analytics requires analytical ability, the capacity to use fairly advanced statistical techniques such as multiple regression analysis, and the ability to appreciate which of the many factors affecting the employment and performance of people are significant enough to merit special treatment.

TIPS

- Ensure that any data collected and analysed is accurate, reliable and relevant.

- Identify those aspects of people management that are critical to organizational success and establish what data is available or can be made available to measure the impact and effectiveness of these aspects.

- Start by instituting processes for the collection and analysis of descriptive analytics and progress to more sophisticated techniques of multidimensional and predictive analytics.

Problem-solving skills 15

Problem solving is the process of analysing and understanding a situation that is creating concern or calls for a solution, diagnosing its cause, and deciding on what should be done to solve the problem and prevent it being repeated. This chapter is set out under the following headings:

1 The nature of problem solving
2 The approach to problem solving
3 The process of problem solving
4 Problem-solving skills
5 Tips

The nature of problem solving

Problem solving is a constant feature of life in organizations and elsewhere. It is something that people professionals do all the time. A logical approach is desirable but this is not easy – the situations where problems have to be solved are often messy, with conflicting evidence, lack of data and political and emotional issues affecting those involved. But even if it is difficult always to apply neat, logical and sequential methods, the principles of getting and analysing what information is available, considering alternatives and making the best choice based on the evidence, an analysis of the context and an assessment of the possible consequences, remain the same. Decision making as considered in the next chapter is an outcome of problem solving.

The approach to problem solving

You will often have to react to problems as they arise, but as far as possible a proactive approach is desirable, involving anticipating potential problems and dealing with them in advance by taking preventative action. Proactive problem solving will probably require creative thinking.

Problems and opportunities

It is sometimes said that 'there are no problems, only opportunities'. This is not universally true, but it does emphasize the point that a problem should lead to positive thinking about what is to be done now, rather than to recriminations. If a mistake has been made, the reasons for it should be analysed to ensure that it does not happen again. And it can be said that it is not enough to solve problems; you must produce creative alternatives.

An analytical approach

A complicated situation needs to be resolved by separating the whole into its component parts. Such an analysis should relate to facts, although, as Peter Drucker (1955) pointed out, when trying to understand the root causes of a problem you may have to start with an opinion. Even if you ask people to search for the facts first, they are quite likely to look for those facts that fit the conclusion they have already reached (what is called in logic 'affirming the consequent').

Opinions are a perfectly good starting point as long as they are brought out into the open at once and then tested against reality. Analyse each hypothesis and pick out the parts that need to be studied and tested (analytical skills are covered in Chapter 11). The 'law of the situation' as formulated by Mary Parker Follett (1924) should govern all problem-solving activities. This states that the logic of facts and events rules in the end.

A creative approach

A strictly logical answer to the problem may not be the best one. Creative thinking is often necessary to develop an entirely new approach.

A simple approach

One of the basic principles of problem solving is known as Occam's razor. It states that 'entities are not to be multiplied without necessity'. In other words, always believe the simplest of several explanations.

Focus on implementation

A problem has not been solved until the decision has been implemented. It is necessary to think carefully not only about how a thing is to be done (by whom, with what resources and by when) but also about what will happen when it is put into effect – its impact on the organization and the people concerned and the extent to which they will cooperate. Unforeseen consequences can upset the most carefully prepared plans.

Involve people

Problems involving people need to be solved by people. Less cooperation will be obtained if solutions are imposed. You impose your answer to a problem. It is best to arrange things so that everyone arrives jointly at a solution, freely agreed to be the one best suited to the circumstances in accordance with the law of the situation.

The process of problem solving

The 12 steps of problem solving are:

1 *Define the situation* – identify the question or difficulty calling for a solution or creating concern.

2 *Specify objectives* – define what is to be achieved now or in the future to deal with an actual or potential problem or a change in circumstances.

3 *Develop hypotheses* – develop hypotheses about what has caused the problem.

4 *Get the facts* – find out what has actually happened and contrast this with an assessment of what ought to have happened. This is easier said than done. Insidious political factors may have contributed to the problem and could be difficult to identify and deal with. The facts may not be clear cut. They could be obscured by a mass of conflicting material. There may be lots of opinions but few verifiable facts. Remember that people will see what has happened in terms of their own position and feelings (their framework of reference). Try to understand the political climate and the attitudes and motivation of those concerned. Bear in mind that, as Jeffrey Pfeffer (1996) commented, 'smart organizations occasionally do dumb things'. Obtain information about internal or external constraints that affect the situation.

5 *Analyse the facts* – determine what is relevant and what is irrelevant. Diagnose the likely cause or causes of the problem. Do not be tempted to focus on symptoms rather than root causes. Test any assumptions. Distinguish between opinions and facts. Dig into what lies behind the problem.

6 *Identify possible courses of action* – spell out what each involves.

7 *Evaluate alternative courses of action* – assess the extent to which they are likely to achieve the objectives, the cost of implementation, any practical difficulties that might emerge and the possible reactions of stakeholders. Consider possible consequences. Critical evaluation techniques, as described in Chapter 12, can be used for this purpose.

8 *Weigh and decide* – determine which alternative is likely to result in the most practical and acceptable solution to the problem. This is often a balanced judgement.

9 *Decide on the objective* – set out goals for implementation of the decision.

10 *Adopt a 'means-end' approach where appropriate* – in complicated situations with long-term implications it may be useful to identify the steps required and select an action at each step that will progressively move the process closer to the goal.

11 *Plan implementation* – prepare a timetable and identify and assemble the resources required.

12 *Implement* – monitor progress and evaluate success. Remember that a problem has not been solved until the decision has been implemented. Always work out the solution to a problem with implementation in mind.

Problem-solving skills

By far the most important problem-solving skill is analytical ability – the capacity to understand complex situations and deconstruct information into smaller and more easily assimilated categories in order to draw conclusions. Analytical skills include logical reasoning, critical thinking, and being able to examine a complex situation and break it down to its constituent but inter-related parts in order to understand it. The other important skill is the ability to base problem solving on systems thinking – a comprehensive analytical approach to understanding how different elements interact within a system, as described in Chapter 17.

TIPS

- *Be systematic* – when the decision is about how to deal with a problem, adopt a problem-solving approach as described above. When it is concerned with some form of innovation, creative thinking may be required to identify what can be. But even then, a logical approach to deciding *how* it should be done is desirable.

- *Think before you act* – this could be a recipe for delay, but decisive people use their analytical ability to come to swift conclusions about the nature of the situation and what should be done about it.

- *Be careful about assumptions* – we have a tendency to leap to conclusions and seize on assumptions that support our case and ignore the facts that might contradict it.

- *Learn from the past* – build on your experience. But don't rely too much on precedents. Situations change.

- *Consult* – involve interested parties in discussions on what needs to be done to obtain their views and convince them that a decision is acceptable.

- *Consider the potential consequences* – McKinsey calls this 'consequence management'. Every decision has a consequence, and you should consider very carefully what that might be and how you will manage it. When making a decision it is a good idea to start from where you mean to end – define the end result and then work out the steps needed to achieve it.

- *Expect the unexpected* – you are then in the frame of mind needed to respond decisively to a new situation.

- *Talk it through* – before you finalize a significant decision talk it through with someone who is likely to disagree so that any challenge they make can be taken into account (but you have to canvass opinion swiftly).

- *Think implementation* – plan how to implement the decision with care. Ensure that the resources required will be available and that the programme of work is realistic.

References

Drucker, P (1955) *The Practice of Management*, London, Heinemann

Follett, M P (1924) *Creative Experience*, New York, Longmans Green

Pfeffer, J (1996) When it comes to 'best practices', why do smart organizations occasionally do dumb things? *Organizational Dynamics*, Summer, pp 33–44

Decision-making skills 16

Decision making is essentially about making choices, often in conditions of uncertainty. This involves analysing a situation or problem, seeking opinions and facts, identifying possible courses of action, weighing them up, defining the preferred action, implementing it and evaluating its effectiveness. Decision-making theory provides a background to the process of decision-making and the skills required. Decision making is considered in this chapter under the following headings:

- Decision-making theory
- The decision-making process
- Decision-making skills
- Tips

Decision-making theory

Decision-making theory as developed by Simon (1979) explains that a rational approach to making a decision requires a logical sequence of steps: (1) analysing the situation, (2) developing possible courses of action, (3) exercising choice and (4) assessing the outcome of the choice. But in accordance with Simon's concept of 'bounded rationality', people do not always have complete information, and the ability to make an optimal choice is therefore limited. Furthermore, what is done in organizations with the evidence depends largely on the context in which it is done. Cultural, social and political factors influence perceptions and judgements, and the extent to which people behave rationally is limited by their capacity to understand the complexities of the situation they are in and by their emotional reactions to it.

The decision-making process

The doyen of management thinkers, Peter Drucker (1955, 1967), observed that:

> A decision is a judgement. It is a choice between alternatives. It is rarely a choice between right and wrong. It is at best a choice between almost right and probably wrong – but much more often a choice between two courses of action neither of which is probably more nearly right than the other.

He also noted that:

> A good deal of decision making tends to centre on problem-solving, that is, on giving answers. And that is the wrong focus. Indeed, the most common source of mistakes in management decisions is the emphasis on finding the right answer rather than the right question... One has to start out with what is right rather than what is acceptable (let alone who is right) because one always has to compromise in the end.

He argued that the best decisions emerge from conflicting viewpoints and that you should not expect or even welcome a bland consensus view. He stated that 'The first rule in decision-making is that one does not make a decision unless there is disagreement. You can benefit from a clash of opinion to prevent falling into the trap of starting with the conclusion and then looking for the facts that support it.' He emphasized that 'The understanding that underlies the right decision grows out of the clash and conflict of divergent opinions and out of the serious consideration of competing alternatives.'

Decision-making skills

Decisive people come to a rapid understanding of the characteristics of the situation in which a decision has to be made and of the factors that affect that situation and therefore their choice of action. This requires analytical ability but also the capacity to see the bigger picture Once they have made up their minds, they do not prevaricate and stick with their chosen course of action.

TIPS

- *Define the problem* – as Drucker (1955) emphasized: 'The first job in decision-making is to find the real problem and to define it.'

- *Avoid procrastination* – it is easy to put an email demanding a decision into the 'too difficult' section of your actual or mental in-tray. Avoid the temptation to fill your time with trivial tasks so that the evil moment when you have to address the issue is postponed. Make a start. Once you have got going you can deal with the unpleasant task of making a decision in stages. A challenge often becomes easier once we have started dealing with it. Having spent five minutes on it we don't want to feel it was time wasted, so we carry on and complete the job.

- *Expect the unexpected* – you are then in the frame of mind needed to respond decisively to a new situation.

- *Think before you act* – this could be a recipe for delay, but decisive people use their analytical ability to come to swift conclusions about the nature of the situation and what should be done about it.

- *Be careful about assumptions* – we have a tendency to leap to conclusions and seize on assumptions that support our case and ignore the facts that might contradict it.

- *Learn from the past* – build on your experience in decision making; what approaches work best. But don't rely too much on precedents. Situations change. The right decision last time could well be the wrong one now.

- *Be systematic* – adopt a rigorous problem-solving approach.

- *Talk it through* – before you make a significant decision talk it through with someone who is likely to disagree so that any challenge they make can be taken into account (but you have to canvass opinion swiftly).

- *Leave time to think it over* – swift decision making is highly desirable but you must avoid knee-jerk reactions. Pause, if only for a few minutes, to allow yourself time to think through the decision you propose to make. And confirm that it is logical and fully justified.

- *Consider the potential consequences* – this is called 'consequence management'. Every decision has a consequence, and you should consider very carefully what that might be and how you will manage it. When making a decision it is a good idea to start from where you mean to end – define the end result and then work out the steps needed to achieve it.

References

Drucker, P (1955) *The Practice of Management*, Heinemann, London
Drucker, P (1967) *The Effective Executive*, Heinemann, London
Simon, H A (1979) Rational decision making in business organizations, *American Economic Review*, **69** (4), pp 493–513

Systems thinking skills   17

Systems thinking, or systemic thinking, is an analytical approach to understanding how different elements interact within a system. It is considered in this chapter under the following headings:

1 The nature of systems thinking

2 The importance of systems thinking

3 Systems thinking techniques

4 The approach to systems thinking

5 Tips

The nature of systems thinking

As described by the Government Office for Science (2023), a system is a set of elements or parts interconnected in such a way that they produce their own pattern of behaviour over time. Wikipedia defines a system as 'a group of interacting or inter-related elements that act according to a set of rules to form a unified whole'. Surrounded and influenced by its environment, a system is described by its boundaries.

A key premise of systems thinking is that large-scale systems change can only be sustained if the entrenched patterns that drive the system are changed. Systems thinking is a framework for seeing the interconnections in a system and a discipline for seeing and understanding the relevant aspects of the whole system – the 'structures' that underlie complex situations. It views a problem as a collection of components or parts that interact and change in response to different interventions, i.e., a system. If we change one part of a system, we are likely indirectly or directly to affect another part. Systems thinking is a way of making sense of the complexity of the world by looking at it in terms of relationships rather than just splitting it down into its parts. It has been used as a way of exploring and developing effective action in complex contexts, enabling systems change. It is necessary to consider how these changes can take place and the impact they will make on each other and the end result. It is also necessary to identify and engage with others in the system and build a shared understanding of it so that changes are coherent and more likely to succeed.

The importance of systems thinking

The CIPD's Profession Map (2022) states that people professionals should understand how to apply systemic thinking to a range of people practices and appreciate that 'an organisation is a whole system, and that your work and actions have an impact elsewhere'. It is pointed out that:

> It's particularly important that people professionals think in a systemic way: understanding how to align the different elements of the organisation's system (for example, the values, the culture, structures, people practices and policies) to maximise the organisation's performance.

The Government Office for Science (2022) stated that:

> Systems thinking is applicable to all civil servants delivering good policy making. It is valuable and applicable when work is strategic but also when it is more reactionary and fast-paced. It helps to create the conditions in which innovative ideas can emerge. This is important when developing legislation, regulation, standards but also at times of crisis, when the way forward isn't always clear or obvious.

Systems thinking means that problems are examined more completely and accurately before acting. By identifying the underlying structures and relationships that drive events and patterns of behaviour it is possible to clarify and expand the choices available and create better long-term solutions. Systems thinking has been described as a language for talking about the complex, interdependent issues managers face every day.

Systems thinking techniques

Systems thinking techniques are used to increase understanding of a system and the relationships within it. They make use of context diagrams, system flow charts, causal loop diagrams and 'pig' models.

Context diagrams

It is necessary to understand the context in which a system functions in order to create a framework within which it can be analysed. This can be done with a context diagram as illustrated in Figure 17.1.

In this example of a context diagram, an analysis is made under four headings (the concentric rings) of the context within which resourcing policies and practices for obtaining the required skills are developed:

- *Under direct control* – policy and practice in recruitment and learning and development.

- *Able to influence* – provide support and encouragement for local and national training and skills development initiatives.

- *Not able to influence but important* – supply of people in labour market, availability and take-up of training.

- *Environmental factors* – impact of Brexit on labour supply; government policies on immigration.

Figure 17.1   A context diagram

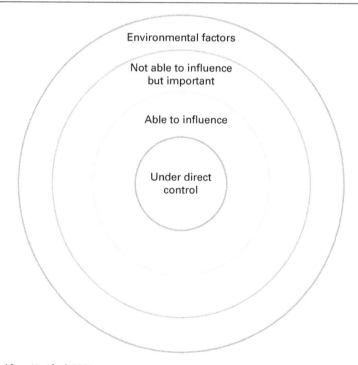

Adapted from Hostford, 2020

System flow charts

System flow charts map each of the elements in the system and their inter-relationships. The example given in Figure 17.2 of a reward system traces the flow of the activities between the starting point – business or corporate strategy – and the ultimate aim – to support the achievement of the organization's business and social purpose. Between these points the chart illustrates how the system's elements are linked together and contribute to the eventual achievement of its aims.

This shows that the management of a reward system requires decisions on how jobs should be valued, the design and operation of pay structures, levels of pay, how pay should progress, the use of bonuses and the choice of benefits. Such decisions can be complex and difficult, especially those concerned with performance pay and bonuses. It clarifies the fundamental

Figure 17.2 A reward system

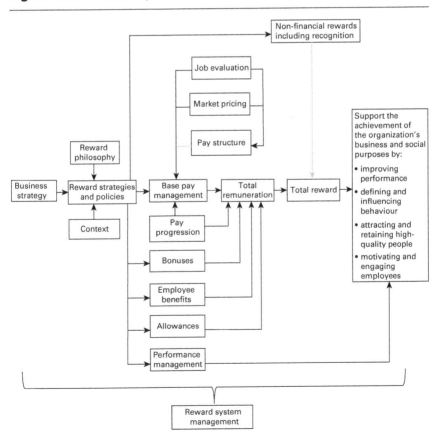

importance of base pay management and indicates how a 'total reward' policy (treating reward as an integrated and coherent whole in order to maximize its impact) emerges from its components.

Causal loop diagrams

A causal loop diagram is a visual representation of how the key variables in a system (factors, issues, processes) are connected and how these interconnections affect each other and the wider system. Causal loop diagrams can be thought of as sentences that are constructed by identifying those variables (the 'nouns') and indicating the causal relationships between them via links (the 'verbs'). By linking together several loops, a concise story can be created about a problem or issue.

A causal loop diagram consists of the elements of the problem or issue shown as loops, the links between the elements, the signs on the links (which show how the variables are interconnected) and the sign of the loops (which shows what type of behaviour the system will produce). By representing a problem or issue from a causal perspective, it is possible to become more aware of the structural forces that affect behaviour. An example is shown in Figure 17.3.

In the example given in Figure 17.3, the first loop is a 'reinforcing loop' designated by an R. It indicates with an 'S' that this aspect of the system shows the potential for an increase in the relevant factor in the loop, i.e. performance. The second loop is called a 'balancing loop' which produces oscillation or movement towards equilibrium. An 'S' would indicate that the direction is positive while an 'O', as in this example, suggests that it might be negative. A summary narrative of how the system is thought to be

Figure 17.3   A causal loop diagram

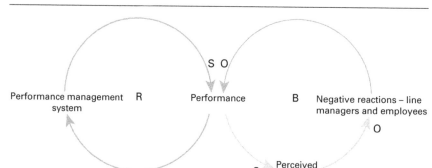

functioning would state that the introduction of a performance manage-ment system should improve performance but that the behaviour of other parts of the system – managers and employees – could reduce its impact. Something has to be done to reduce this perceived threat if the performance management system is to achieve its purpose.

Additional loops can be added to a causal loop diagram. In this instance these could include alternative way of improving performance such as performance pay, learning and development programmes and programmes for enhancing engagement. These loops would explore the interconnections between the various activities, how they could contribute and the issues that might be met in any planned system developments. But causal loop diagrams can sometimes become incredibly complex and therefore self-defeating.

First, remember that less is better. Start small and simple; add more ele-ments to the story as necessary. Show the story in parts. The number of ele-ments in a loop should be determined by the needs of the story and of the people using the diagram. A simple description might be enough to stimulate dialogue and provide a new way to see a problem. In other situations, you may need more loops to clarify the causal relationships you are surfacing.

Loops are shorthand descriptions of what we perceive as current reality; if they reflect that perspective, they are 'right' enough.

Figure 17.4 A 'pig' model

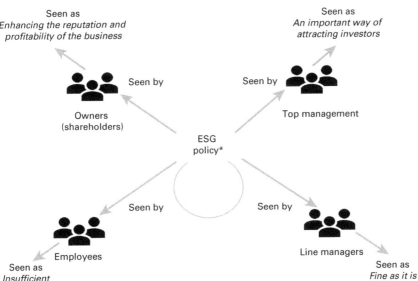

*An ESG (environment, social and governance) policy describes what an organization intends to do to meet its obligations for sustainability, social purpose and how it is managed.

The pig model

Systems thinking means not only looking at the specific elements of the system but also considering the reactions and opinions of the different people who are involved in or with it and therefore affect how it functions. These are the system's stakeholders and consist of the owners (shareholders in a commercial business) or governing body, top management, line managers and employees generally. Their views can be analyzed and recorded in a 'pig' model (so-called because it was first used in an issue concerning pigs).

The approach to systems thinking

In its most basic form, systems thinking should be undertaken at any time when an innovation is under consideration. It is necessary to answer the usual questions such as: what is the evidence that makes this innovation necessary? What is its objective? How will that be achieved? How will we know that it has been successful? But there is a further question – how will this innovation affect other parts of the system? And when asking this last question it is necessary to bear in mind that a system is not only a collection of inter-related activities taking place within the context in which the organization exists, but also a number of people who are involved in those activities. This means that account must be taken of the views of these stakeholders.

System thinking is something individuals should do but it is particularly important and likely to be more effective if it is conducted by teams of people, for example joint management and employee teams. Typical steps that can be taken either by individuals or teams are set out below:

1 Establish the key issues. This may include the need to respond to a new demand or situation or the undesirability of the present arrangements. If a team is involved, the aim is to achieve a shared understanding of the issue or problem.

2 Create a narrative of how the system produces what it does.

3 Take into account the characteristic of the existing system, define the objectives of any initiatives considered necessary to deal with the issues.

4 Gather any evidence revealing the nature of the situation or arrangements including the elements of the system in which the latter take place.

5 Analyse the context within which the proposed innovation is to take place using a *context diagram*.

6 Identify the elements of the system within that context and how they are inter-related. A complex system and the relationships within it can be described in a systems *flow chart*.

7 Construct a *causal loop diagram* to gain a greater understanding of the relationships in a system including how they affect each other and the people involved.

8 Use a *pig model* to analyse the perceived reactions of stakeholders to the proposed innovation.

9 Summarize the outcomes of the above steps and draw up an action programme that takes account of the systems implications they have identified.

10 Implement the action programme and evaluate its effectiveness

---

TIPS

- Remember that systems thinking is particularly powerful when applied to complex problems. Problems are complex when they cannot be solved in a simple linear fashion and require an understanding of the interactions between multiple different elements.

- Use systems thinking to gain insight into how others may see a system differently.

- Bear in mind that evidence is crucial to understand a system.

- Do not overestimate the importance of a part of the system because of an abundance of available data or likewise underestimate the importance of a part of the system due to a lack of data.

- Note that any choices made will have an impact on other parts of the system.

- Identify and engage with others in the system and build a shared understanding of how it operates and how it will be affected by the proposed innovation to ensure that any changes are coherent and likely to succeed.

References

CIPD (2022) Explore the Profession Map, https://www.cipd.org/uk/the-people-profession/the-profession-map/explore-the-profession-map/ (archived at https://perma.cc/D5PL-VDAW)

Government Office for Science (2023) Systems Thinking: An introductory toolkit for civil servants, London, GOV.UK, https://www.gov.uk/government/publications/systems-thinking-for-civil-servants/toolkit (archived at https://perma.cc/AW5N-FN93)

Hostford, J (2020) Finding a Way into Systems, GOV.UK, https://systemsthinking.blog.gov.uk/author/james-hostford/ (archived at https://perma.cc/B7DQ-EV75)

Digital skills   18

This chapter considers the skills required by people professionals in promoting digital transformation within organizations. It is set out under the following headings:

1 Digital people management defined

2 Digital transformation

3 Digital applications for people management

4 The digital roles of the people management function

5 The skills required

6 Tips

Digital people management defined

Digital people management is the use of digital technologies in the form of web-based applications including human resource information systems, cloud technologies, and technologies such as artificial intelligence (AI), social media and smartphones. It involves converting information from a physical form into a digital one (digitization) and using that to facilitate business and people management processes (digitalization).

'Digital' is strictly defined as the representation of values as discrete numbers (1 and 0) rather than as a continuous spectrum. More generally, the term covers anything to do with computers (and smartphones in that they work as computers), how they function and how they are used. Digital technology is concerned with computer-based applications and solutions. These include artificial intelligence (AI) – the science of training machines to perform human-like tasks so that certain functions can be automated.

Digital transformation

Digital transformation is what happens when organizations successfully take advantage of the opportunities offered by digital technology. The aim is to achieve digital maturity – the integration of digital technology into all areas of the business and its acceptance as a way of life. It is not just about its development and introduction. It is also about the ability of people to adapt to the new circumstances. This means changing their mindset and ensuring that they have the understanding and skills required.

Digital transformation will not be achieved unless innovations meet the needs of both the organization and the people working in it. The reasons for and the implications of proposed new digital technology should be communicated to and discussed with those affected by it. Those directly involved should be given the opportunity in good time to learn the necessary skills.

Digital applications for people management

The main uses of digital people management (its 'functionalities') are administration, processing people data, communications and as an aid in recruitment and selection, learning and development and reward activities.

Administration (processing people data)

People management administration is about maintaining a database containing the personal details of individual employees and their employment, pay and benefits, attendance, holiday, performance appraisal, training and disciplinary records. It includes payroll administration and the administration of employee benefits.

Communications

Digital people management improves the capacity of organizations to communicate to their employees and of employees to communicate with their employers and each other. This is done through social media and chatbots. Organizations can operate an enterprise social network (ESN), also known as an internal social network, that functions in the same way as social networks such as Facebook.

Social media uses digital technologies that allow people to connect with each other to create and share information. It involves an online digital platform or website (a social networking site) that enables people to interact via instant messaging (real-time, direct text-based communication between two or more people using smartphones, personal computers, laptops or tablets).

Chatbots are an AI facility that can be embedded in a messaging application. They can be used to answer queries by employees on such matters as holiday and maternity leave entitlement, information on terms and conditions of employment or work problems. Chatbots are either accessed through virtual assistants such as Google Assistant and Amazon Alexa, or via messaging apps such as Facebook Messenger or WeChat.

Learning and development

Digital learning includes the use of e-learning and learning platforms and the development of virtual learning environments. Digital resources and techniques include the use of smartphones and learning apps, social media, enterprise social networks, web searches for knowledge acquisition, virtual and augmented reality and online courses. Generative AI applications such as ChatGPT – GPT stands for generative pre-trained transformer – produce text for learning and other purposes including subject outlines, detailed content, exercises and notes for facilitators. AI can also be used to help employees find appropriate learning material.

Recruitment and selection

AI can be used to sift CVs, profile existing high performers and apply their traits to candidates, write role profiles that eliminate biased language and remove all trace of protected characteristics from applications.

Chatbots can provide candidates with immediate help and answer their questions about the job or application process. This allows recruiters to engage with candidates more effectively and save time by automating routine tasks. They can sift and rank candidates based on their written applications. Interviews can be scheduled.

Reward

AI can be used to analyse performance data to provide better information for reward decisions. Internal and external reward information can identify discrepancies and trends over time thus helping to address pay inequity. Information can be obtained on the relative value of different elements of employees' benefit packages and how they are used so that employees are able to make informed choices.

The digital roles of the people management function

The people management function has three roles in digital management and transformation. First, it can assess the scope for the use of digital processes, especially AI, and help to introduce them. Second, it can help to promote digital transformation through learning and information programmes. And third, it can take steps to mitigate the potentially damaging effects of digitalization, especially AI.

The skills required

Like any other professional, people professionals need to have basic digital skills such as word processing, using the simpler spreadsheet formulae and preparing PowerPoint slides. To play their full part in digital transformation, they should also have analytical skills and the ability to visualize how digital, especially AI applications, can benefit the organization but also the problems they may create. They need digital skills such as confidence in using dashboards and the ability to produce prompts for the use of AI-powered language models such as ChatGPT as a means of generating human-like text based on context and past conversations.

TIPS

- Be clear on how you want to use digital technology.
- Consider how the technology will impact jobs and the way things are done.
- Consult with employees to identify unforeseen risks and gain buy-in.
- Scrutinize products before procurement to understand how technical functions work and what ongoing management is available.
- Communicate to applicants and employees how technology is used.
- Start small and pilot the approach when using AI. By adopting it in low-risk, low-complexity tasks, organizations can build trust and experience with AI before deciding whether to invest in larger-scale projects.
- Allow for testing, learning and refinement in the early stages of procurement and installation in order to build confidence in the approach and ensure organizational and people needs are met.

Statistical skills   19

People professionals need skills in using statistics in order to analyse and present quantitative information (people analytics) that can be used to guide decisions as a support to evidence-based management, and to monitor outcomes. Statistics are an essential element in human capital management and are also important in such fields as performance management (the analysis of appraisal results and levels of performance) and reward management (the analysis of market rates, pay reviews, the distribution of pay and equal pay). Statistics also play a major part in the analysis of surveys and research evidence. This chapter summarizes the basic statistical techniques under the following headings:

1 The nature of statistics

2 Frequency

3 Measures of central tendency

4 Measures of dispersion

5 Correlation

6 Regression

7 Causality

8 Tests of significance

9 Testing hypotheses

10 Tips

The nature of statistics

Statistics describe and summarize data relating to a 'population', i.e. a homogeneous set of items with variable individual values. This involves measuring frequencies, central tendencies and dispersion. Statistics can also measure the relationships between variables (correlation and regression), establish the relation between cause and effect (causality), assess the degree of confidence that can be attached to conclusions (tests of significance) and

Figure 19.1   Examples of charts

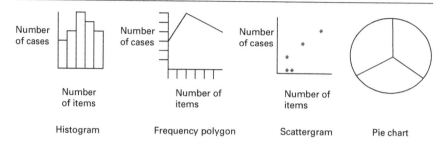

test hypotheses (the chi-squared test and null-hypothesis testing). They can form the basis for a projection – an estimate or forecast of a future situation based on a study of present trends.

Statistics can be expressed in tabular form or graphically using data visualization techniques. A wide variety of software is available to conduct the more sophisticated analyses. People professionals do not need advanced statistical skills unless they are conducting or taking part in detailed research projects. This chapter describes the statistics or statistical concepts that they are most likely to use or should be familiar with, namely those concerned with frequency, measures of central tendency, dispersion, correlation, regression, causality, tests of significance and testing hypotheses.

Frequency

Frequency is the number of times individual items in a population or set occur. It is represented in frequency distributions. The messages conveyed by the analysis of frequency can be conveyed most effectively by using data visualization techniques such as the graphs illustrated in Figure 19.1.

Measures of central tendency

Measures of central tendency identify the middle or centre of a set of data. There are three types:

- Arithmetic average or mean – the total of items or scores in a set divided by the number of individual items in the set. It may give a distorted picture because of large items at either end of the scale.

- Median – the middle item in a range of items (often used in pay surveys when the arithmetic mean is likely to be distorted).
- Mode – the most commonly occurring item in a set of data.

Measures of dispersion

Measures of dispersion assess the extent to which the items in a set are dispersed or spread over a range of data. This can be done in five ways:

1 By identifying the upper quartile or lower quartile of a range of data. The strict definition of an upper quartile is that it is the value that is exceeded by 25 per cent of the values in the distribution, and the lower quartile is the value below which 25 per cent of the values in a distribution occur. More loosely, especially when looking at pay distributions, the upper and lower quartiles are treated as ranges rather than points in a scale and represent the top and the bottom 25 per cent of the distribution respectively.

2 By presenting the total range of values from top to bottom; this may be misleading if there are exceptional items at either end.

3 By calculating the inter-quartile range, which is the range between the value of the upper quartile and that of the lower quartile. This can present more revealing information of the distribution than the total range.

4 By calculating the standard deviation, which is used to indicate the extent to which the items or values in a distribution are grouped together or dispersed in a normal distribution, i.e. one that is reasonably symmetrical around its average. As a rule of thumb, two-thirds of the distribution will be less than one standard deviation from the mean, 95 per cent of the distribution will be less than two standard deviations from the mean, and less than 1 per cent of the distribution will be more than three standard deviations from the mean.

5 By calculating variance, which is the square of a standard deviation.

Correlation

Correlation represents the relationship between two variables. A variable is a factor called a 'dependent variable' that may be affected by changes in an 'independent variable' (sometimes called the 'predictor variable'). If the independent and dependent variables are strongly connected to one another, they are highly correlated and vice versa. In statistics, correlation is measured by the coefficient of correlation, which varies between -1 and +1 to indicate totally negative and totally positive correlations respectively. A correlation of zero means that there is no relationship between the variables. Establishing the extent to which variables are correlated is an important feature of people management research in, for example, assessing the degree to which a performance management system improves organizational performance. But correlations are no more than associations – they do not indicate causal relationships. Multiple correlation looks at the relationship between more than two variables.

Regression

Regression is another way of looking at the relationship between independent and dependent variables. It expresses how changes in levels of one item relate to changes in levels of another. The levels may be expressed in the form of correlations. A regression line (a trend line or line of best fit) can be traced on a scattergram expressing values of one variable on one axis and values of the other variable on another axis, as shown in Figure 19.2.

A trend line like this can be drawn by hand as a line of best fit, but it can be calculated mathematically with greater accuracy. The distances of points from the trend line (the residuals) can be calculated as a check on the reliability of the line.

Figure 19.2   A scattergram with regression (trend) line

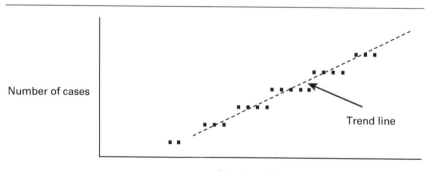

Number of cases

Trend line

Number of items

Where there are two or more independent variables that might affect the dependent variable, multi-regression analysis can be used. If there are two or more dependent variables as well as two or more independent variables, multivariate analysis is used. Multiple regression analysis involves complex calculations and is best conducted with the aid of software such as SPSS.

Causality

Causality is the representation of cause and effect, i.e. the link between independent and dependent variables. To establish causality is to explain how one thing leads to another. Causality is a major issue in research, especially in the people management field. It may be relatively easy to establish correlations in the shape of a demonstration that X is associated with Y; it is much more difficult and sometimes impossible to prove that X causes Y. There are a number of reasons for this, of which the two set out below are the most important.

First, complications arise because of the phenomenon of multiple causation. There may be a number of factors contributing to a result. Researchers pursuing the holy grail of trying to establish what people management contributes to an organization's performance are usually confronted with a number of reasons why an organization has done well in addition to adopting 'best practice HRM', whatever that is. Statistical techniques can be used to 'control' some variables, i.e. eliminate them from the analysis, but it is difficult if not impossible to ensure that people management practices have been completely isolated and that their direct impact on the organization's performance has been measured. Multivariate analysis is used where there is more than one dependent variable and where the dependent variables cannot be combined.

Second, there is the phenomenon of reverse causation, when a cause may be pre-dated by an effect – A might have caused B but, alternatively, B might have come first and be responsible for A. For example, it is possible to demonstrate that organizations with effective performance management schemes do better than those without. But it might equally be the case that it is high-performing organizations that introduce effective performance management. It can be hard to be certain.

Tests of significance

Significance as a statistical concept refers to the degree to which an event could have occurred by chance. At the heart of statistical science lies a simple idea, which is that the chance or probability of various patterns of events can be predicted. When a particular pattern is observed it is possible to work out what the chances of its occurrence may be, given our existing state of knowledge or by making certain assumptions. If something has been observed that is unlikely to have occurred by chance, this occurrence can be accepted as significant. The problem is that any attempt to reach general conclusions may have to rely on fragmentary data. It is usually necessary to rely on samples of the population being studied and all sampling is subject to experimental error – the result can only be expressed in terms of probability and confidence limits will have to be placed on it. These can be calculated in terms of the standard error that might be expected from a sample. A standard error is the estimated standard deviation of a sample mean from a true mean. This implies that on approximately 95 per cent of occasions the estimate of the mean provided by the sample will be within two standard errors of the true mean.

Testing hypotheses

The *chi-squared test* uses a statistical formula to test a hypothesis by assessing the degree of agreement between the data actually obtained and that expected under a particular hypothesis.

A *null hypothesis* is a method of hypothesis testing frequently used by researchers in which it is assumed that there is no relationship between two or more variables. It asks the question: 'Could the hypothetical relationship have been caused by chance?' If the answer is 'no', then the hypothesis is worth pursuing. However, it does not prove that the hypothesis is correct; it only indicates that something is worth further investigation. It can be associated with the chi-squared test.

TIPS

- Use statistical techniques to add weight to assumptions about the causes and relationships of events.

- Take care to assemble good data (i.e. realistic and relevant) as the basis for statistical analysis.

- Select the statistical technique with care – it should be the one that is most likely to be able 'to tell the story', given the existence of appropriate and accurate data.

- Do not confuse correlation with causation.

- Remember that there may be a number of reasons for a causal relationship or correlation and be aware of the phenomenon of reverse causation.

- Where possible, illustrate findings with visual representations – graphs, diagrams etc.

Research skills   20

People specialists and those studying for people management professional qualifications may be involved in conducting or taking part in research projects. Postgraduate students usually do so. The purpose of this chapter is to describe the skills and techniques used in research and explain what they need to use in planning and conducting research projects. It is set out under the following headings:

1 The nature of research

2 Processes involved in research

3 Research methodology

4 Methods of collecting data

5 Planning and conducting research programmes

6 Tips

The nature of research

The conduct of research has been described as follows:

> Researchers collect and analyse data, develop hypotheses, replicate and extend earlier work, communicate their results with others, [and] review and critique the results of their peers (Committee on Science, Engineering and Public Policy, 1995).

Research is concerned with establishing what is and from this predicting what will be. It does not decide what ought to be; that is for people interpreting the lessons from research in their own context. Research is about the conception and testing of ideas and hypotheses. This is a creative and imaginative process, although new information is normally obtained within the framework of existing theory and knowledge. Logic and rational argument are methods of testing ideas after they have been created.

What emerges from research is a theory – a well-established explanatory principle that has been tested and can be used to make predictions of future developments. Kurt Lewin (1945) wrote that 'Nothing is as practical as a good theory'. A 'good' theory is produced by the clear, logical and linear development of an argument with a close relationship between information, hypothesis and conclusion. Quality of information is a criterion for good research, as is the use of critical evaluation techniques.

The production of narratives that depict events (case studies) or the collection of data through surveys are elements in research programmes, but they can stand alone as useful pieces of information that illustrate practice. Research can be quantitative or qualitative and be based on a philosophy of positivism or phenomenology.

Quantitative research

Quantitative research is empirical – based on the collection of factual data, which is measured and quantified. It answers research questions from the viewpoint of the researcher. It may involve a considerable amount of statistical analysis, using methods for collecting the data through questionnaires, surveys, observation and experiments. The collection of data is distinct from its analysis.

Qualitative research

Qualitative research aims to generate insights into situations and behaviour so that the meaning of what is happening can be understood. It emphasizes the interpretation of behaviour from the viewpoint of the participants. It is based on evidence that may not be easily reduced to numbers. It makes use of interviews, case studies and observation but it may also draw on the information obtained from surveys. It may produce narratives or 'stories' describing situations, events or processes.

Positivism

Positivism is the belief that researchers should focus on facts (observable reality), look for causality and fundamental laws, reduce phenomena to their simplest elements (reductionism), formulate hypotheses and then test them. Researchers are objective analysts. The emphasis in positivism is on quantifiable observations that lend themselves to statistical analysis. It tends to be deductive, i.e. it uses logical reasoning to reach a conclusion based on established evidence or premises.

Phenomenology

Phenomenology focuses on the meaning of phenomena rather than the facts associated with them. Researchers adopting this philosophy try to understand what is happening. Their approach is holistic, covering the complete picture, rather than reductionist. Researchers collect and analyse evidence, but their purpose is to use this data to develop ideas that explain the meaning of things. They believe that reality is socially constructed rather than objectively determined. Using a phenomenological approach means that the research unfolds as it proceeds – early evidence is used to indicate how to move on to the next stage of evidence collection and analysis, and so on. It tends to be inductive, i.e. general laws are inferred from particular instances.

Processes involved in research

Research involves the following logical, analytical and critical thinking processes: deduction, induction, hypothesis testing, grounded theory, paradigms and critical evaluation.

Deduction

Deduction uses logical reasoning to reach a conclusion that necessarily follows from defined premises. If the premises are correct, so is the deduction. The conclusion is therefore contained within the evidence. Deduction is not a creative or imaginative argument that produces new ideas.

Induction

Induction is the process of reaching generalized conclusions from the observation of particular instances. In contrast to deduction, inductive conclusions may be tentative but they contain new ideas. In research, both deductive and inductive reasoning can be used in hypothesis testing.

Hypothesis testing

Formulating a hypothesis is an important element in a research project in that it provides a basis for the development of a theory and the collection and analysis of data. A hypothesis is a supposition – a tentative explanation of something. It is a provisional statement that is taken to be true for the purpose of argument or a study and usually relates to an existing wider body of knowledge. A hypothesis has to be tested and should be distinguished from a theory, which is an explanation of something that *has* been tested. A working hypothesis is a general hypothesis that has been operationalized so that it can be tested.

Hypothesis formulation and testing uses the strengths of both deductive and inductive processes; the former entirely conclusive but unimaginative, the latter tentative but creative. Induction produces ideas and deduction tests them.

To test a hypothesis, data has to be obtained that will demonstrate that its predicted consequences are true or false. Simply leaping to the conclusion that a hypothesis is true because a single cause of the consequence has been observed falls into the trap of what logicians call the 'fallacy of affirming the consequent'. There may be alternative and more valid causes. The preferred method of testing is that of denying the consequent. This is 'falsification' as advocated by Popper (1959). His view was that however much data may be assembled to support a hypothesis, it is not possible to reach a conclusive proof of the truth of that hypothesis. Popper therefore proposed that it was insufficient simply to assemble confirmatory evidence; what must also be obtained is evidence that refutes the hypothesis. Only one instance of refutation is needed to falsify a theory, whereas however many confirmations of the theory exist it will still not be proved conclusively.

Grounded theory

Grounded theory is an inductive method of developing the general features of a theory by grounding the account in empirical observations or evidence. The researcher uses empirical evidence directly to establish the concepts and relationships that will be contained in the theory. Evidence is collected from both primary sources (i.e. obtained directly by the researcher from the originator of the evidence) and secondary sources (i.e. information that is already available in the literature or on the internet). Where possible, use is made of triangulation, i.e. information is obtained from more than two sources.

Paradigm

The term 'paradigm' has become popularized as meaning a way of looking at things. It is often used loosely, but properly it means the philosophical and conceptual framework of a scientific school or discipline within which theories, laws and generalizations and the experiments performed in support of them are formulated. In other words, it is a common perspective that underpins the work of theorists so that they use the same approach when conducting research.

Critical evaluation

Critical evaluation involves making informed judgements about the value of ideas and arguments. It uses critical thinking, which is the process of analysing and evaluating the quality of ideas, theories and concepts to establish the degree to which they are valid and supported by the evidence (evidence-based) and the extent to which they are biased. It means reflecting on and interpreting data, drawing warranted conclusions and identifying faulty reasoning, assumptions and biases. A creative leap may be required to reach a judgement.

Research methodology

Research methodology involves the collection and analysis of evidence and testing hypotheses or propositions. The sources of evidence and how they will be accessed will be identified. This will include the analysis of primary and secondary source documents, further literature reviews, interviews, surveys and field work. The methodology can include the use of triangulation, integrative synthesis, cross-lagged analysis, establishing validity, and quantitative or qualitative research.

Triangulation

Triangulation takes place when information is obtained from more than two sources, for example surveys, case studies and literature reviews. Greater confidence can be attached to a result if different methods lead to the same answer. If a researcher uses only one source this may be misleading or random. If two sources are used the results may clash. If three sources are used the hope is that two of the three will produce similar answers, or if three clashing answers are produced, the researcher knows that the question needs to be reframed, methods reconsidered, or both.

Integrative synthesis

Integrative synthesis involves the collection and comparison of evidence involving two or more data collection methods. It investigates patterns across published research studies, compensating for single-study weaknesses in research design to improve the internal and external validity of the various research findings. It relies on the judgment of researchers, but around a structured framework and set of questions.

Cross-lagged models

Cross-lagged models are longitudinal statistical studies in which two or more variables are measured for a large number of subjects at each of several waves or points in time. The variables divide naturally into two sets and the primary purpose of the analysis is to estimate and test the cross-effects between these two sets.

Establishing validity

Validity is the extent to which a concept, conclusion or measurement is well-founded and corresponds accurately to the real world. It is clearly important that research produces valid results – the ultimate aim of all the research methods described in this chapter. There are three ways of assessing validity:

1 *Criterion validity* (or criterion-related validity) measures how well one measure predicts an outcome for another measure. A test has this type of validity if it is useful for predicting performance or behaviour in another situation (past, present or future).

2 *Convergent validity* reflects the extent to which a construct is related to other measures of the same construct (a construct is an idea or theory containing various conceptual elements that can be subjective and not based on empirical evidence).

3 *Discriminant validity* is shown by demonstrating that a construct has low or null relationships with other measures.

Methods of collecting data

The main methods of collecting data are interviews, questionnaires, surveys, case studies, observation, diaries and experimental designs.

Interviews

Interviews are an important research method. They obtain factual data and insights into attitudes and feelings and can take three forms:

1 *Structured*, which means that they obtain answers to a pre-prepared set of questions. This ensures that every topic is covered and minimizes variations between respondents. But they may be too rigid and inhibit spontaneous and revealing reactions.

2 *Unstructured*, which means that no questions have been prepared in advance and the person being interviewed is left free to talk about the subject without interruption or intervention. Such 'non-directive' interviews are intended to provide greater insight into the interviewee's perspective, avoid fitting respondents into predetermined categories and enable interviewers to explore issues as they arise. But they can be inconsequential and lead to poor data that is difficult to analyse.

3 *Semi-structured*, which means that the areas of interest have been predetermined and the key questions to be asked or information to be obtained have been identified. The interviewer may have a checklist but does not follow this rigidly. This approach enables the interviewer to phrase questions and vary their order to suit the special characteristics of each interviewee. It may avoid the problems of the completely structured or unstructured interview but it does require a considerable degree of skill on the part of the interviewer.

Interviews are basically qualitative but they can become more quantitative by the use of content analysis. This records the number of times references are made as recorded in an interview to the key issues or areas of interest it was intended to cover.

The advantages of interviews are that they obtain information directly from people involved in the area being researched and can provide insights into attitudes and perspectives that questionnaires and surveys will not reveal, thus promoting in-depth understanding. They enable the interviewer to probe answers and check that questions had been understood. But the disadvantages are that:

- the construction of the interview questions may result in leading questions or bland answers;
- interviewers may influence the interviewees' reactions by imposing their own reference frame;
- respondents may tell interviewers what they want to hear;

- they are time-consuming – to set up, to conduct and to analyse;
- they require considerable skill, including the abilities to recognize what is important and relevant, to probe when necessary, to listen and to control the interview so that it covers the ground it was intended to cover.

Questionnaires

Questionnaires collect data systematically by obtaining answers on the key issues and opinions that need to be explored in a research project. They are frequently adopted as a means of gathering information on matters of fact or opinion. They use a variety of methods, namely closed questions that require a yes or no answer, ranking in order of importance or value, or Likert scales. The latter, named after Rensis Likert, the American sociologist who invented them, ask respondents to indicate the extent to which they agree or disagree with a statement. For example, in response to a statement such as, 'I like my job' the choice may be 1 strongly agree, 2 agree, 3 disagree, 4 strongly disagree. Alternatively, an extended scale may be used and respondents asked to ring round the number that reflects their view about the statement (the higher the number the greater the agreement). For example: My contribution is fully recognized 1 2 3 4 5 6 7. Extended scales facilitate the quantitative analysis of responses to questionnaires.

To construct and use a questionnaire effectively it is necessary to:

1 Identify the key issues and potential questions.

2 Ensure questions are clear.

3 Avoid asking two questions in one item.

4 Avoid leading questions that supply their own answers.

5 Decide on the structure of the questionnaire including its length (not too many items) and the type of scale to be used.

6 Code questions for ease of analysis.

7 Start with simple factual questions, moving on later to items of opinion or values.

8 Add variety and the opportunity to check consistency by interspersing positive statements such as 'I like working for my boss' with occasional associated negative ones such as 'I do not get adequate support from my boss'.

9 Pilot test the questionnaire.

10 Code results and analyse. Where rating scales have been used the analysis can be quantified for comparison purposes. Content analysis can be used to analyse narrative answers to open-ended questions.

Questionnaires can effectively gather factual evidence but are not so useful for researchers who are investigating how or why things are happening. It is also impossible to assess the degree of subjectivity that has crept in when expressing opinions. For example, people managers may give an opinion of the extent to which a performance-related pay scheme has in fact improved performance but the evidence to support that opinion may be lacking. This is where interviews can be more informative.

Surveys

Surveys obtain information from a defined population of people. Typically, they are based on questionnaires but they can provide more powerful data than other methods by using a combination of questionnaires and interviews and, possibly, focus groups (groups of people gathered together to answer and discuss specific questions). When developing and administering surveys the matters for consideration are:

- The definition of the purpose of the survey and the outcomes hoped for – these must be as precise as possible.

- The population to be covered – this may involve a census of the whole population. Alternatively, if the population is large, sampling will be necessary (see below).

- The choice of methods – relying entirely on questionnaires may limit the validity of the findings. It is better, if time and the availability of finance permit, to complement them with interviews and, possibly, focus groups. Consideration has to be given to the extent to which triangulation (comparing the information obtained from more than two sources) is appropriate.

- The questions to which answers are required, whichever method is used.

- The design of questionnaires and the ways in which interviews or focus groups, if used, should be structured.

- How the outcome of the survey will be analysed and presented, including the use of case studies.

Sampling

In using surveys it may not be feasible to cover the whole population (the sampling frame) and sampling will therefore be necessary. Sampling means that a proportion of the total population is selected for study and the aim is to see that this proportion represents the characteristics of the whole population. The sample must not be biased and that is why in large-scale surveys use is made of random sampling, i.e. the individuals covered by a survey are not selected in accordance with any criteria except that they exist in the population and can be reached by the survey. It is the equivalent of drawing numbers out of a hat. However, if the sample frame is considered to be already arranged randomly as in the electoral roll, then structured sampling, that is, sampling at regular intervals, can be employed.

Sampling can produce varying degrees of error depending on the size of the sample. Statistical techniques can be used to establish sample errors and confidence limits. For example, they might establish that a sampling error is 3 per cent and the confidence limit is 95 per cent. This could be reasonably satisfactory, depending on the nature of the research (medical research aims to achieve 100 per cent confidence).

Case studies

A research case study is a description of a situation or a history of an event or sequence of events in a real-life setting that illustrates a particular area of interest, for example, how a performance management system has been developed and works. In learning and development, case studies are analysed by those involved to learn something by diagnosing the causes of a problem and working out how to solve it.

Case studies are used extensively in people management research as a means of collecting empirical evidence in a real-life context. Information is obtained about a situation, an event or a set of events that establishes what has happened, how it happened and why. Case studies provide information that contributes to the creation of a theory as part of a grounded theory approach, or an established theory to be validated. In addition, they can take the form of stories or narratives that illuminate a decision or a set of decisions, why they were taken, how they were implemented and with what result. They can illustrate a total situation and describe the processes involved and how individuals and groups behave in a social setting.

Case study protocol sets out the objectives of the research, how the case study will support the achievement of those objectives, including the evidence required, and how the work of producing the case study will be conducted. The methodology covers:

- sources of evidence – interviews, observation, documents and records;
- the need to use multiple sources of evidence (triangulation) so far as possible;
- the questions to which answers need to be obtained;
- how the case study should be set up, including informing those involved of what is taking place and enlisting their support;
- the schedule of interviews and other evidence-collection activities;
- how the case study database recording the evidence will be set up and maintained;
- how the case study will be presented – including the chain of evidence so that the reader can follow the argument and trace the development of events, the headings and report guidelines (these may be finalized during the course of the exercise) and whether or not the name of the organization will be revealed on publication (named case studies are more convincing than anonymous ones);
- how approval will be sought for the publication of the case study, especially if it reveals the name of the organization.

Case studies are useful ways of collecting information on the reality of organizational life and processes. But there is a danger of them being no more than a story or an anecdote that does not contribute to greater knowledge or understanding. Much skill and persistence are required from the researcher in gaining support, ensuring that relevant and revealing information is obtained and presenting the case study as a convincing narrative from which valid and interesting conclusions can be derived. All this must be done without taking a biased view, which can be difficult.

Observation

Observation of individuals or groups at work is a method of getting a direct and realistic impression of what is happening. It can be done by a detached or an involved observer, or by participant observation.

Detached observers who simply study what is going on without getting involved with the people concerned may only get a superficial impression of what is happening and may be resented by the people under observation as 'eavesdropping'. Involved observers work closely with employees and can move around, observe and participate as appropriate. This means that they can get closer to events and are more likely to be accepted, especially if the objectives and methods have been agreed in advance.

Participant observation in the fullest sense means that the researcher becomes an employee and experiences the work and the social processes that take place at first hand. This can provide powerful insights but is time-consuming and requires considerable skill and persistence.

The issues with any form of observation are getting close enough to events to understand their significance and then analysing the mass of information that might be produced in order to come up with findings that contribute to answering the research question.

Diaries

Getting people to complete diaries of what they do is a method of building a realistic picture of how people, especially managers, spend their time.

Experimental designs

Experimental designs involve setting up an experimental group and a control group and then placing subjects at random in one or the other group. The conditions under which the experimental group functions are then manipulated and the outcomes compared with the control group, whose conditions remain unchanged. The classic case of an experimental design was the Hawthorne study. This took place in a factory setting and its findings made a major impact on thinking about how groups function and on the human relations movement. But this was exceptional. It is much easier to use experiments in a laboratory setting, which has been done many times with students. But there is always the feeling that such experiments do not reflect real-life conditions.

Planning and conducting research programmes

The steps required to plan and conduct a research programme are:

1. Define research area

This should be one that interests the researcher and has a clear link to an accepted theory or an important issue worth exploring. The research should generate fresh insights into the topic. It is necessary to undertake background reading at this stage by means of a preliminary review of the literature (particularly academic journals but also books, especially those based on research) to identify what has already been achieved in this area and any gaps (academic articles often include proposals on further research). The context within which the research is to be carried out needs to be explained and justified.

2. Formulate initial research question

This provides a rationale for the research. It is in effect a statement that answers the questions: 'What is this research project intended to address and what is its potential contribution to increasing knowledge?' At this stage it is based on the outcome of the initial work carried out in step 1, but it will be refined and reformulated at a later stage when more information about the research has been made available.

3. Review literature

A literature review will focus mainly on academic journals. The aim is to establish what is already known about the topic, identify existing theoretical frameworks and find out what other relevant research has been carried out.

4. Develop theoretical framework

It is necessary to conduct the research within a clear theoretical framework. This will set out the models, concepts and theories that can be drawn on and developed to provide an answer to the research question. If an appropriate framework does not exist, a grounded theory approach may be required in which the researcher uses empirical evidence directly to establish the concepts and relationships that will be contained in the theory adopted as the research framework. It is important to be clear about the assumptions, conditions and limitations that impinge on the investigation.

5. Finalize the research question

The initial research question needs to be finalized in the light of the outcome of the earlier steps. The final research question will identify the issues to be explored and the problems to be investigated. It will include a statement of intent, which will set out what the research is to achieve. This statement leads to the formulation of the hypotheses or propositions that will be tested by survey or experiment during the research programme.

6. Formulate hypotheses or propositions

A hypothesis provisionally states a relationship between two concepts in such a way that the consequences of the statement being true can be tested. Hypotheses (there may be more than one) indicate the form the research project will take in the shape of obtaining and analysing the evidence required to test them. Hypotheses may be attached to the statement of the research question. A proposition is a proposal put forward as an explanation of an event, a possible situation or a form of behaviour that will be tested by the research.

7. Design the research

This means considering initially what research philosophy will be adopted. Is it to be positivist, phenomenological, or both? It is then necessary to establish the methodology. A decision will need to be made as to the extent to which the research will be quantitative, qualitative or, again, a combination of the two and on the methods to be used.

8. Draw up research programme.

This will cover how the research will be conducted, the timetable and the resources (funding, people, software, etc.) required. Careful project planning is essential.

9. Prepare and submit proposal

This will justify the research by setting out the research question, the proposed methodology, and how the research is intended to increase knowledge and understanding. It will also describe the programme and the resources required.

10. Conduct the research project

This includes obtaining and analysing the evidence from the various sources needed to answer the research question and prove or disprove hypotheses. The significance of the findings in relation to the research question and the hypotheses will be discussed and reference will be made to relevant information provided in the literature. This involves an extended literature review, data collection, the use of logical, analytical and critical thinking processes and the use of statistical analysis where relevant.

11. Develop conclusions

These draw together all the evidence. They provide the answer to the research question and explain why hypotheses have been accepted or rejected. The significance of the findings will also be assessed in terms of how they contribute to the development of existing knowledge and understanding. Any limitations to the study should also be mentioned.

12. Make recommendations

These set out any guidelines emerging from the research. They may also indicate any follow-up actions required if the research has been conducted within an organization.

TIPS

- Formulate a research question that clearly indicates the reason(s) for the proposed research and the advantages that will result from its conclusion, and will provide a sense of direction to the whole project.
- Consider adopting a grounded theory approach by basing the account on empirical observations or evidence.
- Use triangulation to extend the range of sources of information.

- Prepare a detailed programme describing methods, time scales and how resources will be deployed.
- Review and describe any practical implications emerging from the research.

References

Committee on Science, Engineering and Public Policy (1995) *On Being a Scientist: Responsible conduct in research*, Washington DC, National Academy of Sciences, National Academy of Engineering, Institute of Medicine

Lewin, K (1945) The research centre for group dynamics at Massachusetts Institute of Technology, *Sociometry*, 8, pp 126–36

Popper, K (1959) *The Logic of Scientific Discovery*, London, Hutchinson

PART FOUR
Personal skills

Communicating skills 21

People professionals spend much of their time communicating to management, their line manager colleagues, employees, candidates and outside bodies and advisors. As described in the next three chapters, communicating involves the effective use of the spoken and written word and active listening. But it is also necessary to understand the basic skills required for any form of communication. These skills are needed to ensure that the message you want to deliver gets across clearly and that you understand the significance of any messages you receive. This is not always easy. There are a number of barriers to communication that need to be understood and dealt with to ensure that communications are effective. This chapter covers communication skills under the following headings:

1 Barriers to communication

2 Tips

Barriers to communication

Words may sound or look precise, but they are not. All sorts of barriers exist between the communicator and the receiver. Unless the following barriers are overcome the message will be distorted or will not get through; tips on how to do this are given at the end of the chapter.

Hearing what we want to hear

What we hear or understand when someone speaks to us is largely based on our own experience and background. Instead of hearing what people have told us, we hear what our minds tell us they have said. We have preconceptions about what people are going to say, and if what they say does not fit into our framework of reference, we adjust it until it does.

Ignoring conflicting information

We tend to ignore or reject communication that conflicts with our own beliefs. If it is not rejected, some way is found of twisting and shaping its meaning to fit our preconceptions.

When a message is inconsistent with existing beliefs, the receiver rejects its validity, avoids further exposure to it, easily forgets it or, in his or her memory, distorts what has been heard.

Perceptions about the communicator

It is difficult to separate what we hear from our feelings about the person who says it. Non-existent motives may be ascribed to the communicator. If we like people we are more likely to accept what they say – whether it is right or wrong – than if we dislike them.

Influence of the group

The group with which we identify influences our attitudes and feelings. What a group hears depends on its interests. Workers are more likely to listen to their colleagues, who share their experiences, than to outsiders such as managers or union officials.

Words mean different things to different people

Essentially, language is a method of using symbols to represent facts and feelings. Strictly speaking, we can't convey meaning – all we can do is to convey words. Do not assume that because something has a certain meaning to you it will convey the same meaning to someone else.

Non-verbal communication

When we try to understand the meaning of what people say, we listen to the words but we also use other clues that convey meaning. We attend not only to what people say but to how they say it. We form impressions from what is called body language – eyes, the shape of the mouth, the muscles of the face, even posture.

We may feel that these tell us more about what someone is really saying than the words he or she uses. But there is enormous scope for misinterpretation.

Emotions

Our emotions colour our ability to convey or to receive the true message. When we are insecure or worried, what we hear seems more threatening than when we are secure and at peace with the world. When we are angry or depressed, we tend to reject what might otherwise seem like reasonable requests or good ideas.

In a heated argument, many things that are said may not be understood or may be badly distorted.

Noise

Any interference to communication is 'noise'. It can be literal noise that prevents the message being heard, or figurative in the shape of distracting or confused information that distorts or obscures the meaning.

Size

The larger and more complex the organization, the greater the problem of communication. The more levels of management and supervision a message has to pass through, the greater the opportunity for distortion or misunderstanding.

TIPS

- Adjust to the world of the receiver – try to predict the impact of what you are going to write or say on the receiver's feelings and attitudes. Tailor the message to fit the receiver's vocabulary, interests and values. Be aware of how the information might be misinterpreted because of prejudices, the influence of others and the tendency of people to reject what they do not want to hear.

- Use feedback – get a message back from the receiver that tells you how much has been understood.

- Use face-to-face communication – in any fairly complex situation or when the communication is about a difficult issue, whenever possible talk to people rather than email or write to them. That is how you get feedback. You can adjust or change your message according to reactions. You can also deliver it in a more human and understanding way – this can help to overcome prejudices. Verbal criticism can often be given in a more constructive manner than a written reproof, which always seems to be harsher. But remember that face-to-face communication is a two-way process. You are communicating to someone but they are also communicating to you. Listening skills are required to ensure that this process works.

- Use reinforcement – you may have to present your message in a number of different ways to get it across. Re-emphasize the important points and follow up.

- Use direct, simple language – this seems obvious, but many people clutter up what they say with jargon, long words and elaborate sentences.

- Use different channels – some communications have to be in writing to put the message across promptly and without any variations in the way they are delivered. But, wherever possible, supplement written communications with the spoken word. Conversely, an oral briefing should be reinforced in writing.

- Suit the actions to the word – communications have to be credible to be effective. There is nothing worse than promising the earth and then failing to deliver. When you say you are going to do something, do it. Next time you are more likely to be believed.

- Reduce problems of size – convince management of the benefits of reducing the number of levels in the hierarchy

- Encourage a reasonable degree of informality in communications. Ensure that activities are grouped together to ease communication on matters of mutual concern.

- Select the method of communication according to the nature of the message and the recipients. Simply providing information is not sufficient; it has to be sent in a form that will elicit the desired response.

Report-writing skills 22

The ability to express oneself clearly on paper and to write effective reports is one of a people manager's most important skills. As often as not, it is through the medium of reports that you will convey your ideas and recommendations to your line manager and colleagues and inform them of the progress you are making. This chapter is set out under the following headings:

1 What makes a good report?

2 Structure

3 Presentation

4 Tips

What makes a good report?

The purposes of a report are to analyse and explain a situation, and/or to propose and gain agreement to a plan. It should be logical, practical, persuasive and succinct.

To be an effective report writer you must clearly start by having something worthwhile to say. Your analysis of opinions and facts and your evaluation of options should provide a base for positive conclusions and recommendations.

Structure

A report should have a beginning, a middle and an end. If the report is lengthy or complex it will also need a summary of conclusions and recommendations. There may also be appendices containing detailed data and statistics.

Beginning

Your introduction should explain why the report has been written, its aims, its terms of reference, and why it should be read. It should then state the sources of information upon which the report was based. Finally, if the report is divided into various sections, the arrangement and labelling of these sections should be explained.

Middle

The middle of the report should contain the facts you have assembled and your analysis of those facts. The analysis should lead logically to a diagnosis of the causes of any problem with which the report is concerned. The conclusions and recommendations included in the final section should flow from the analysis and diagnosis. The most common weakness in reports is that the facts do not lead naturally to the conclusions or the conclusions are not supported by the facts.

Summarize the facts and your observations. If you have identified alternative courses of action, set out the pros and cons of each, but make it quite clear which one you favour. Don't leave your readers in mid-air.

A typical troubleshooting report would start by analysing the present situation; it would then diagnose any problems or weaknesses in that situation, explaining why these have occurred before making proposals on ways of dealing with the problem.

End

The final section of the report should set out your recommendations, stating how each of them will help to achieve the stated aims of the report or overcome any weaknesses revealed by the analytical studies.

The benefits and costs of implementing the recommendations should then be explained. The next stage is to propose a firm plan for implementing the proposals – the programme of work, complete with deadlines and names of people who would carry it out. Finally, tell the recipient(s) of the report what action, such as approval of plans or authorization of expenditure, you would like them to take.

Summary

In a long or complex report it is very helpful to provide an executive summary of conclusions and recommendations. It concentrates the reader's mind and can be used as an agenda in presenting and discussing the report. It is useful to cross-reference the items to the relevant paragraphs or sections of the report.

Presentation

The way in which you present your report affects its impact and value. The reader should be able to follow your argument easily and not get bogged down in too much detail.

Paragraphs should be short and each one should be restricted to a single topic. If you want to list or highlight a series of points, tabulate them or use bullet points. For example:

Pay reviews

Control should be maintained over increments by issuing guidelines to managers on:

- the maximum percentage increase to their payroll allowable for increments to individual salaries;
- the maximum percentage increase that should be paid to a member of staff.

Paragraphs may be numbered for ease of reference. Some people prefer the system that numbers main sections 1, 2, etc., subsections 1.1, 1.2, etc., and sub-sub-sections 1.1.1, 1.1.2, etc. However, this can be clumsy and distracting. A simpler system, which eases cross-referencing, is to number each paragraph, not the headings, 1, 2, 3, etc.; sub-paragraphs or tabulations are identified as 1(a), 1(b), 1(c), etc. and sub-sub-paragraphs if required (avoid if possible) as 1(a)(i), 1(a)(ii), 1(a)(iii), etc. (or use bullet points).

Use headings to guide people on what they are about to read and to help them to find their way around the report. Main headings should be in capitals or bold and subheadings in lower case or italics.

A long report could have an index listing the main and subheadings and their paragraph numbers like this:

Table 22.1   Reporting index

	Paragraphs
PAY ADMINISTRATION	83–92
Pay structure	84–88
Job evaluation	89–90
Pay reviews	91–92

Your report will make most impact if it is brief and to the point. Read and re-read your draft to cut out any superfluous material or flabby writing. Use but don't over-use bullet points to simplify the presentation and to put your messages across clearly and succinctly.

Do not clutter up the main pages of the report with masses of indigestible figures or other data. Summarize key statistics in compact, easy-to-follow tables with clear headings. Relegate supporting material to an appendix.

TIPS

- Use plain words to convey your meaning. Don't use unnecessary adjectives and adverbs. Don't use roundabout phrases where single words would serve. Use familiar, easily understood words with a precise meaning rather than vague ones. Avoid jargon. Do not include too many multi-syllable words.

- Keep your sentences simple and short – not too many sub-clauses.

- Remember the importance of good, clear presentation of material.

- Structure the report clearly and logically.

Speaking skills   23

A people manager's job often includes giving formal or informal presentations at meetings or addressing groups of people at conferences or training sessions. To be able to speak well in public is therefore a necessary skill that you should acquire and develop.

The keys to effective speaking as covered in this chapter are:

1 Overcoming nervousness

2 Preparation

3 Delivery

4 Using PowerPoint

5 Tips

Overcoming nervousness

Some nervousness is a good thing. It makes you prepare, makes you think and makes the adrenalin flow, thus raising performance. But excessive nervousness ruins your effectiveness and must be controlled.

The common reasons for excessive nervousness are fear of failure, fear of looking foolish, fear of breakdown, a sense of inferiority and dread of the isolation of the speaker. To overcome it there are three things to remember and six things to do.

Three things to remember about nervousness

1 Everyone is nervous. It is natural and, for the reasons mentioned, a good thing.

2 Speaking standards are generally low. You can do better than the other person.

3 You have something to contribute. Otherwise, why should you have been asked to speak?

Six things to do about nervousness

1 Practise. Take every opportunity you can get to speak in public. The more you do it, the more confident you will become. Seek constructive criticism and act on it.

2 Know your subject. Get the facts, examples and illustrations that you need to put across.

3 Know your audience. Who is going to be there? What are they expecting to hear? What will they want to get out of listening to you?

4 Know your objective. Know what you want to achieve. Visualize, if you can, each member of your audience going away having learned something new that he or she is going to put into practical use.

5 Prepare.

6 Rehearse.

Preparation

Allow yourself ample time for preparation in two ways. First, leave yourself plenty of low-pressure time; start thinking early – in your shower, on the way to work, while mowing your lawn, any place where you can freely develop new ideas on the subject. Second, you should leave yourself lots of time to actually prepare the talk. There are eight stages of preparation.

1. Agreeing to talk

Do not agree to talk unless you know you have something to contribute to the particular audience on the particular subject.

2. Getting informed

Collect facts and arguments for your talk by reading up on the subject, talking to colleagues and friends, keeping cuttings and files on subjects you may have to speak on, and writing down all the points as they occur.

3. Deciding what to say

Start by defining your objective. Is it to persuade, inform, interest or inspire? Then decide the main message you want to put across. Adopt the 'rule of three'. Few people can absorb more than three new ideas at a time. Simplify your presentation to ensure that the three main points you want to convey come over loud and clear. Finally, select the facts and arguments that best support your message.

Never try to do too much. The most fatal mistake speakers can make is to tell everything they know. Select and simplify using the rule of three.

4. Structuring your presentation

Good structure is vital. It provides for continuity, makes your thoughts easy to follow, gives the talk perspective and balance and, above all, enables you to ram your message home.

The classic method of structuring a talk is to 'Tell them what you are going to say – say it – tell them what you have said'. This is the rule of three in action again. The attention span of most people is limited. Your audience will probably only listen to one-third of what you say. If you say it three times in three different ways, they will at least hear you once.

You were probably told at school that an essay should have a beginning, a middle and an end. Exactly the same principle applies to a talk.

Tackle the middle of your talk first and:

- write each main message on a separate postcard;
- list the points you want to make against each main message;
- illustrate the points with facts, evidence and examples, and introduce local colour;
- arrange the cards in different sequences to help you to decide on the best way to achieve impact and a logical flow of ideas.

Then turn to the opening of your talk. Your objectives should be to create attention, arouse interest and inspire confidence. Give your audience a trailer to what you are going to say. Underline the objective of your presentation – what they will get out of it.

Finally, think about how you are going to close your talk. First and last impressions are very important. End on a high note.

Think carefully about length, reinforcement and continuity. Never talk for more than 40 minutes at a time; 20 to 30 minutes is better. Very few speakers can keep people's attention for long. An audience is usually very interested to begin with (unless you make a mess of your opening), but interest declines steadily until people realize that you are approaching the end. Then they perk up. Hence the importance of your conclusion.

To keep their attention throughout, give interim summaries that reinforce what you are saying and, above all, hammer home your key points at intervals throughout your talk.

Continuity is equally important. You should build your argument progressively until you come to a positive and overwhelming conclusion. Provide signposts, interim summaries and bridging sections that lead your audience naturally from one point to the next.

5. Prepare your notes

Your notes will be based on what you have already prepared. If you are giving a talk without the use of PowerPoint you can record your notes (the main messages and the supporting bullet points) on postcards so that they can easily be referred to in your presentation. It is often a good idea to write out your opening and closing remarks in full and then learn them by heart so that you can begin and end confidently. Clearly, they both have to be succinct.

If you are using PowerPoint (most people do), the text on the slides should correspond to the main points you want to make, with the proviso that you do not overload the slides (see penultimate section in this chapter). You can then print the PowerPoint slides full size and use them as your notes, with some brief and easily read annotations if you need them. The slides can also serve as handouts. Audiences are accustomed to these and no longer expect lots of prose, which they don't read anyhow.

At conferences handouts are often issued in advance. This can be slightly disconcerting to the speaker, as members of the audience may bury their heads in the handouts and appear to be paying little attention to what is being said. Some speakers insist on the handouts being issued after the presentation, but this is not always allowed by the conference organizer. In these circumstances, it is up to you to make what you say as interesting as possible so the audience does pay attention.

6. Prepare visual aids

As your audience will only absorb one-third of what you say, if that, reinforce your message with visual aids. Appeal to more than one sense at a time. PowerPoint slides provide good backup, but don't overdo them and keep them simple. Too many visuals can be distracting, and too many words, or an over-elaborate presentation, will distract, bore and confuse your audience.

7. Rehearse

Rehearsal is vital. It instils confidence, helps you to get your timing right, enables you to polish your opening and closing remarks and helps you to coordinate your talk and visual aids.

Rehearse the talk to yourself several times and note how long each section takes. Get used to expanding your notes without waffling. Never write down your talk in full and read it during rehearsal. This will guarantee a stilted and lifeless presentation.

Practise giving your talk out loud – standing up, if that is the way you are going to present it. Some people like to record themselves but that can be off-putting. It is better to get someone to hear you and provide constructive criticism. It may be hard to take but it could do you a world of good.

Finally, try to rehearse in the actual room in which you are going to speak, using your visual aids and with someone listening at the back to make sure you are audible.

8. Check and prepare arrangements on site

Check the visibility of your visual aids. Make sure that you know how to use them. Test the projector. Brief your projector operator and get them to run through the slides to ensure there are no snags.

Be prepared for something to go wrong with your equipment. You may have to do without it at short notice; that is why you should not rely too much on visual aids.

Before you start your talk, check that your notes and visual aids are in the right order and to hand. There is nothing worse than a speaker who mixes up their speech and fumbles helplessly for the next slide.

Delivery

With thorough preparation you will not fail. You will not break down. But the way you deliver the talk will affect the impact you make. Good delivery depends on technique and manner.

Technique

Your *voice* should reach the people at the back. If you want to know that you are being heard, ask. It is distracting if someone shouts 'speak up'. Don't speak too fast. Vary the pace, pitch and emphasis of your delivery. Pause before making a key point, to highlight it, and again afterwards to allow it to sink in. Try to be conversational. Avoid a stilted delivery. This is one reason why you should never read your talk. If you are your natural self the audience is more likely to be on your side.

Light relief is a good thing if it comes naturally. People are easily bored if they feel they are being lectured at, but you should never tell jokes unless you are good at telling jokes. Don't drag them in because you feel you must. Many effective and enjoyable speakers never use them.

Your *words* and *sentences* should be simple and short.

Your *eyes* are an important link with your audience. Look at them, measure their reaction and adjust to it. Don't fret if people look at their watches; it's when they start shaking them to see if they've stopped that you should start to worry!

Use *hands* for gesture and emphasis only. Avoid fidgeting. If you have any pockets, don't put your hands in them.

Stand naturally and upright, not too casually. Be and look like someone in command. If you pace up and down like a caged tiger you will distract your audience. They will be waiting for you to trip over some equipment or fall off the edge of the platform.

Manner

Relax and show that you are relaxed. Convey an air of quiet confidence. Relaxation and confidence will come with thorough preparation and practice. At the beginning of your presentation look around at the audience and smile at them.

Don't preach or pontificate to your audience. They will resent it and turn against you.

Show sincerity and conviction. Obvious sincerity, belief in your message, positive conviction and enthusiasm in putting your message across count more than any technique.

Using PowerPoint

Most speakers rely on PowerPoint to back up their presentations. The slides are easy to prepare and, because they enforce the use of bullet points, they encourage the development of succinct and easily followed expositions and arguments. They also enable handouts to be easily produced. But PowerPoint slides can be over-used, and present a number of dangers that can reduce rather than enhance the impact of a presentation. The following are 10 guidelines on their preparation and use:

1 Don't use too many slides. It's very tempting as they are so easy to prepare, but if they proliferate they can divert the attention of the audience from the key points you want to make (remember the rule of three). In a 40-minute presentation you should aim to keep the number of slides down to 15 or so – never more than 20. And the number should be reduced pro rata for shorter talks.

2 Don't clutter up the slides with too many words. The rule of six should be adopted – no more than six bullet points and no more than six words per bullet point. Keeping slides down to this number concentrates the mind wonderfully.

3 Make the font size as large as possible (another good reason for keeping the number of words to a minimum). Try to ensure that the heading is not less than 32 points and the text not less than 24 points. Ensure that the text can be seen against whatever background you select (yellow text on a deepish blue background stands out quite well).

4 Use diagrams wherever you can, on the basis that every picture can tell a story better than a host of words. Diagrams break up the presentation. There is nothing more boring than a succession of slides that are entirely bullet-pointed.

5 Use the PowerPoint facility for cascading bullet points (custom animation/ appear) with discretion. It offers the advantage of making sure that each point can be dealt with in turn and is thus given greater significance. If all the points are displayed at once the audience will be tempted to read it as a whole rather than listening to each point separately. But cascading every list of bullet points can bore and distract the audience. Save this approach for slides in which you have to elaborate on each point separately. Also use the other PowerPoint facilities with discretion. The 'fly' facility provides a variation in the way in which bullet points are presented to an audience. It is also helpful if you want to build up a diagram or flow chart to emphasize the sequence of points, but overdoing it can be messy and create confusion. It is tempting to use the 'dissolve' facility to provide elegant variation, but again, it can simply distract an audience who have come to hear what you have to say rather than to be present at a demonstration of PowerPoint tricks.

6 Do not try to be either too slick or too clever. Consultants often make this mistake when making presentations to clients. They attempt to overwhelm their audience with an over-sophisticated presentation and the people subjected to it are not impressed. They may prefer presenters who can get their points across without being propped up by PowerPoint – it shows that they can express themselves without recourse to a visual aid. There is often a reaction against over-slick or clever-clever presentations.

7 PowerPoint slides provide useful notes, but don't just read them out point by point. Your audience may well ask themselves the question: 'What's the use of listening to this person who is simply telling me something that I can equally well read?'

8 It is sometimes a good idea to show a slide with a series of bullet points and give the audience the chance to read it. Then elaborate as necessary or, better still, get some participation by encouraging them to make comments or ask questions.

9 Never use the pre-packaged PowerPoint presentations. It always shows and it reveals the speaker as someone who cannot think of anything original to say. Never use other people's slides. You need to present your own ideas, not theirs.

10 Rehearse using the slides (or the handouts if you do not have a projector) to ensure that you can elaborate as necessary, and to indicate where you might get the audience to read them, with follow-up questions from yourself. You must be quite clear about the sequence of slides, and it is a good idea to prepare bridging remarks in advance to link slides together. A succession of unconnected slides will not impress.

TIPS

- Learn to become an effective speaker with practice. Seize every opportunity to develop your skills.
- Control nervousness with preparation and knowledge of technique.
- Prepare thoroughly – it's half the battle.
- Use technique to help you exploit your personality and style to the full, not to obliterate them.
- Rehearse, rehearse, rehearse. Practice, practice, practice.

Listening skills   24

People professionals spend a lot of time listening. They need to develop the listening skills required to ensure that this time is well spent; that it provides insight and information on any issues that are being discussed. This chapter is set out under the following headings:

1 The importance of listening

2 Why people don't listen

3 Effective listening

4 Tips

The importance of listening

Most of us filter the spoken words addressed to us so that we absorb only some of them – frequently those we want to hear. Listening is an art that not many people cultivate. But it is a very necessary one, because a good listener will gather more information and achieve better rapport with the other person. And both these effects of good listening are essential to good communication. It is important to know why people don't listen and what effective listeners do so that you can avoid these pitfalls yourself.

Why people don't listen

People don't listen properly because they are:

- unable to concentrate, for whatever reason;
- too preoccupied with themselves;
- over-concerned with what they are going to say next;
- uncertain about what they are listening to or why they are listening to it;
- unable to follow the points or arguments made by the speaker;
- simply not interested in what is being said.

Effective listening

Effective listeners concentrate on the speaker, following not only words but also body language, which, through the use of eyes or gestures, often underlines meaning and gives life to the message. They respond appropriately to points made by the speaker, if only in the shape of encouraging grunts. They ask questions to elucidate meaning and to give the speaker an opportunity to rephrase or underline a point. They comment on the points made by the speaker without interrupting the flow in order to test understanding and demonstrate that the speaker and listener are still on the same wavelength. They are alert at all times to the nuances of what the speaker is saying.

TIPS

- Give the speaker your undivided attention, Put aside distracting thoughts.
- Acknowledge what is being said to you. Look at the speaker directly.
- Reflect back on what is being said with remarks such as 'What I'm hearing is...' and 'Sounds like you are saying...'.
- Use your body language and gestures to convey your attention.
- Let the speaker go on with the minimum of interruption.
- Do not slump in your chair – lean forward, show interest and maintain contact by means of body language

Influencing skills

25

Influencing skills and techniques are used to get people to do something you want them to do. This might be just seeing your point of view or taking action, or even getting them to do nothing. People professionals are in the business of influencing people. They have to persuade senior management, line managers and employees to accept their advice or proposals. Influencing involves case presentation and may require the submission of a business case. This chapter is set out under the following headings:

1 Persuading people

2 Case presentation

3 Making a business case

4 Tips

Persuading people

Persuasion is akin to selling. You may feel that good ideas should sell themselves, but life is not like that. People resist change and anything new is usually treated with suspicion. Here are 10 rules for effective persuasion:

1 *Define your objective and get the facts.* If you are persuading someone to agree to a proposal, first decide what you want to achieve and why. Assemble all the arguments and facts you need to support your case. Eliminate emotional arguments so that you and others can judge the proposition on the facts alone.

2 *Define the problem.* If there is a problem to resolve and you are trying to persuade someone to accept your views on what should be done about it, first decide whether the problem is a misunderstanding (a failure to understand each other accurately) or a true disagreement (a failure to agree even when both parties understand one another). It is not necessarily

possible to resolve a true disagreement by understanding each other better. People generally believe that an argument is a battle to understand who is correct. More often, it is a battle to decide who is more stubborn.

3 *Find out what the other party wants.* The key to all persuasion is to see your proposition from the other person's point of view. Find out how they look at things. Establish what they need and want.

4 *Accentuate the benefits.* Present your case in a way that highlights the benefits to the other party or at least reduces any objections or fears.

5 *Predict the other person's response.* Everything we say should be focused on that likely response. Anticipate objections by asking yourself how the other party might react negatively to your proposition and thinking up ways of responding to them.

6 *Create the other person's next move.* It is not a question of deciding what we want to do but what we want the other person to do.

7 *Convince people by reference to their own perceptions.* People decide on what to do on the basis of their own perceptions, not yours.

8 *Prepare a simple and attractive proposition.* Make it as straightforward as possible. Present the case 'sunny side up', emphasizing its benefits. Break the problem into manageable pieces and deal with them one step at a time.

9 *Make the other person a party to your ideas.* Get them to contribute. Find some common ground so that you can start with agreement. Don't try to defeat them in an argument – you will only antagonize them.

10 *Clinch and take action.* Choose the right moment to clinch the proposal – don't prolong the discussion and risk losing it. But follow up promptly.

Case presentation

Persuasion means making a case for what you think should be done. You have to convince people to believe in your views and accept your recommendations. To do this, you must have a clear idea of what you want, and you have to show that you believe in it yourself. Above all, the effectiveness of your presentation will depend upon the care with which you have prepared it.

Thorough preparation is vital. You must think through not only what should be done and why, but also how people will react. Only then can you decide how to make your case, stressing the benefits without underestimating the costs, and anticipating objections. The four steps you should take are:

1 Show that your proposal is based on a thorough analysis of the facts and that the alternatives were properly evaluated before the conclusion was reached. If you have made assumptions, you must demonstrate that these are reasonable on the basis of relevant experience and justifiable projections, which allow for the unexpected. Bear in mind that a proposal is only as strong as its weakest assumption.

2 Spell out the benefits – to the organization and/or the individuals to whom the case is being made. Wherever possible, express benefits in financial terms. Abstract benefits, such as customer satisfaction or workers' morale, are difficult to sell. But don't produce 'funny numbers' – financial justification that will not stand up to examination.

3 Reveal costs. Don't try to disguise them in any way. And be realistic. Your proposition will be destroyed if anyone can show that you have underestimated the costs.

4 Remember, senior management decision makers want to know in precise terms what they will get for their money. Many are likely to be cautious, being unwilling and often unable to take much risk. For this reason, it can be difficult to make a case for experiments or pilot schemes unless the decision maker can see what the benefits and the ultimate bill will be.

Making a business case

You may be asked specifically to produce a business case. This will set out the reasons why a proposed course of action will benefit the business, how it will provide that benefit and how much it will cost. A business case is a particular form of persuasion and all the points made above apply to its preparation and presentation. But there are some special features about business cases, as described below.

A business case is typically made either in added-value terms (i.e. the income generated by the proposal will significantly exceed the cost of implementing it), or on the basis of the return on investment or ROI (i.e. the cost of the investment, say in training, is justified by the financial returns in such areas as increased productivity). Clearly, a business case is more convincing when it is accompanied by realistic projections of added value or return on investment. When people make out a case for capital expenditure they analyse the cash flows associated with the investment and calculate the benefits – in financial terms as far as possible – that are likely to arise from them. The objective is to demonstrate that in return for paying out a given amount of cash today, a larger amount will be received over a period of time.

It can be more difficult to make out a business case for a people management innovation in financial terms. The costs can and should be calculated but the benefits may have to be expressed in qualitative terms. A business case will be enhanced if:

- data is available on the impact the proposal is likely to make on key areas of the organization's operations, e.g. productivity, customer service levels, quality, shareholder value, income generation, innovation, skills development, talent management;

- it can be shown that the proposal will increase the business's competitive edge, for example enlarging the skill base or multi-skilling to ensure that it can achieve competitive advantage through innovation and/or reducing time-to-market;

- there is proof that the innovation has already worked well within the organization (perhaps as a pilot scheme) or represents 'good practice' that is likely to be transferable to the organization;

- it can be implemented without too much trouble, for example not taking up a lot of managers' time, or not meeting with strong opposition from line managers, employees or trade unions (it is as well to check the likely reaction before launching a proposal);

- it will add to the reputation of the company;

- it will enhance the 'employer brand' of the company by making it a 'best place to work';

- the proposal is brief, to the point and well argued – it should take no more than five minutes to present orally and should be summarized in writing on the proverbial one side of one sheet of paper.

Making a business case is obviously easier when management is preconditioned to agree to the proposition. For example, it is not hard to convince top managers that performance-related pay is a good thing – they may well be receiving bonus payments themselves and believe, rightly or wrongly, that because it motivates them it will motivate everyone else. Talent management is another process where top management needs little persuasion that things need to be done to enhance and preserve the talent flow, although they will have to be convinced that, in practice, innovations will achieve that aim.

Performance management may be slightly more difficult because it is hard to demonstrate that it can produce measurable improvements in performance, but senior managers are predisposed towards an approach that at least promises to improve the level of performance.

The toughest area for justification in added-value terms can be expenditure on learning and development. The business case for L&D should demonstrate how learning, training and development programmes will meet business needs. An L&D initiative can be supported by pointing out that one or more of the following benefits would accrue:

- individual, team and corporate performance would improve in terms of output, quality, speed and overall productivity;
- high-quality employees would be attracted by offering them learning and development opportunities, increasing their levels of competence and enhancing their skills, thus enabling them to obtain more job satisfaction, to gain higher rewards and to progress within the organization;
- operational flexibility would be improved by extending the range of skills possessed by employees (multi-skilling).

TIPS

- Decide what you want to achieve and why and then assemble all the arguments and facts that support your case.
- See your proposition from the other person's point of view.
- Emphasize the benefits.
- Show how the proposal will add value.
- Make any proposal brief, to the point and well-argued.

Negotiating skills   26

People professionals who are involved in industrial relations may conduct or take part in negotiations with trade union representatives or officials. They therefore need negotiating skills as dealt with in this chapter under the following headings:

1 The nature of negotiating

2 The process of negotiation

3 Stages of negotiation

4 Negotiating and bargaining skills

5 Tips

The nature of negotiating

Negotiating requires considerable skill. It is a process in which two parties – management and the trade union – get together with the aim of getting the best deal possible for their business or their members. It involves bargaining, which is reaching the most advantageous position in discussion with another party by means of offers and counter-offers.

Negotiations usually involve a conflict of interest. In pay negotiations, unions want the highest settlement they can get; management wants the lowest. In negotiations about other terms and conditions, unions will want the best result for their members while management will want to avoid agreeing to anything other than what they think is reasonable from their viewpoint. It can be a zero-sum game – what one side gains the other loses. No one likes to lose, so there is scope for conflict, which has to be managed if an amicable agreement is to be achieved. And negotiators do, or should, try to end up on friendly terms, whatever differences of opinion have occurred on the way. After all, they may well meet again.

A 'mutual gains' approach is desirable but not always achievable. This involves recognizing that while the interests of the two parties will probably differ in some if not many respects, it may be possible to find common ground. A problem-solving process is best. Both sides exchange information to advance interests that they think will benefit both of them. This results in the generation of options and a choice of those that are considered to provide mutual gains.

The process of negotiation

Negotiating takes place when two parties meet to reach an agreement concerning a proposition, such as a pay claim, one party has put to the other. Negotiation can be convergent when both parties are equally keen to reach a win-win agreement (in commercial terms, a willing buyer/willing seller arrangement). It can be divergent when one or both of the parties aim to win as much as they can from the other while giving away as little as possible. Negotiations in an industrial relations setting differ from commercial negotiations in the respects shown in Table 26.1.

In negotiations on pay or other terms and conditions of service, management represents the employer's interests and employee representatives represent the interests of employees. Both sides are of equal status. Negotiations take place in an atmosphere of uncertainty. Neither side knows how strong the other side's bargaining position is or what it really wants and will be prepared to accept.

Table 26.1 Commercial and industrial relations negotiations compared

Industrial relations negotiations	Commercial negotiations
• Assume an ongoing relationship – negotiators cannot walk away. • The agreement is not legally binding. • Conducted on a face-to-face basis. • Carried out by representatives responsible to constituents. • Make frequent use of adjournments. • May be conducted in an atmosphere of distrust, even hostility.	• Negotiators can walk away. • The contract is legally binding. • May be conducted at a distance. • Carried out directly with the parties being responsible to a line manager. • Usually conducted on a continuing basis. • Usually conducted on a 'willing buyer/willing seller' basis.

Stages of negotiation

Negotiations are conducted in four stages: initial steps, opening, bargaining and closing.

Initial steps

In a pay negotiation, unions making the claim will define for themselves three things: a) the target they would like to achieve, b) the minimum they will accept, and c) the opening claim they believe will be most likely to achieve the target. Employers define three related things: 1) the target settlement they would like to achieve, 2) the maximum they would be prepared to concede, and 3) the opening offer that will provide them with sufficient room to manoeuvre in reaching their target. The difference between a union's claim and an employer's offer is the negotiating range. If the maximum the employer will offer exceeds the minimum the union will accept the difference will be the settlement range, in which case a settlement will be easily reached. If, however, the maximum the employer will offer is less than the minimum the union will accept, negotiations will be more difficult and a settlement will only be reached if the expectations of either side are adjusted during the bargaining stage. The extent to which this will happen depends on the relative power of the two parties. The strength of the arguments put forward by either party will also be a factor, but the major consideration is usually power.

Similarly, in a negotiation on an employment issue such as working arrangements, the union sets out a request (or demand) but usually has a fall-back position, while the employer decides on an initial response but again has a fall-back position.

Preparation for negotiation by either party involves:

- deciding on the strategy and tactics to be used;
- listing the arguments to be used in supporting their case;
- identifying the arguments or counter-arguments the other party is likely to use;
- obtaining supporting data;
- selecting the negotiating team, briefing them on the strategy and tactics and rehearsing them in their roles.

Opening

Tactics in the opening phase of a negotiation are as follows:

- open realistically and move moderately;
- challenge the other side's position as it stands – do not destroy their ability to move;
- observe behaviour, ask questions and listen attentively in order to assess the other side's strengths and weaknesses, their tactics and the extent to which they may be bluffing;
- make no concessions at this stage;
- be non-committal about proposals and explanations – do not talk too much.

Bargaining

After the opening moves, the main bargaining phase takes place in which the gap is narrowed between the initial positions. The attempt is made to persuade each other that their case is strong enough to force the other side to close at a less advantageous point than they had planned. Bargaining is often as much about concealing as revealing – keeping arguments in reserve to deploy when they will make the greatest impact. As far as possible, the basis for an agreement is established; that is, the common ground.

The following tactics are used:

- Always make conditional proposals: 'If you will do this, then I will consider doing that' – the words to remember are: 'if... then ...'.
- Never make one-sided concessions: always trade off against a concession from the other party: 'If I concede x, then I expect you to concede y'.
- Negotiate on the whole package: negotiations should not allow the other side to pick off item by item (salami negotiation).
- Keep the issues open to extract the maximum benefit from potential trade-offs.

There are certain bargaining conventions that experienced negotiators follow because they appreciate that by so doing, they create the atmosphere of trust and understanding that is essential to the sort of stable bargaining relationship that benefits both sides. Some of the more generally accepted conventions are as follows:

- Whatever happens during the bargaining, both parties are hoping to reach a settlement.

- While it is preferable to conduct negotiations in a civilized and friendly manner, attacks, hard words, threats and controlled losses of temper may be used by negotiators to underline determination to get their way and to shake their opponent's confidence and self-possession. But these should be treated by both sides as legitimate tactics and should not be allowed to shake the basic belief in each other's integrity or desire to settle without taking drastic action.

- Off-the-record discussions ('corridor negotiations') can be mutually beneficial as a means of probing attitudes and intentions and smoothing the way to a settlement, but they should not be referred to specifically in formal bargaining sessions unless both sides agree in advance.

- Each side should be prepared to move from its original position.

- It is normal, although not inevitable, for the negotiation to proceed by alternate offers and counter-offers from each side, leading steadily towards a settlement.

- Third parties should not be brought in until both sides agree that no further progress can be made without them.

- Concessions, once made, cannot be withdrawn.

- If negotiators want to avoid committing themselves to 'a final offer' with the risk of devaluing the term if they are forced to make concessions, they should state as positively as they can that this is as far as they can go. Bargaining conventions allow further moves from this position on a *quid pro quo* basis.

- Firm offers must not be withdrawn.

- The final agreement should mean exactly what it says. There should be no trickery and the agreed terms should be implemented without amendment.

- So far as possible the final settlement should be framed and communicated in such a way as to reduce the extent to which the other party loses face or credibility.

Figure 26.1 Negotiating range with a settlement zone

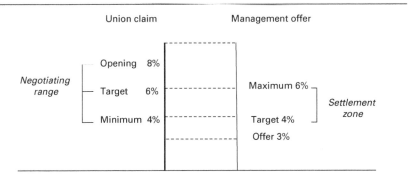

Figure 26.2 Negotiating range without a settlement zone

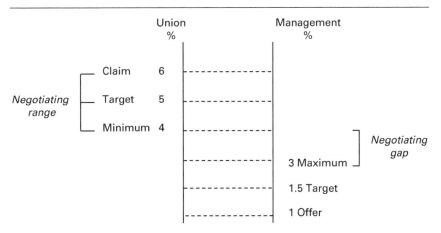

The features of typical negotiations are illustrated in Figures 26.1 and 26.2. In the example shown in Figure 26.1, the chance of settlement without too much trouble is fairly high. It is when the employer's maximum is less than the union's minimum, as shown in Figure 26.2, that the trouble starts.

Closing

There are various closing techniques:

● Make a concession from the package which is traded off against an agreement to settle. The concession can be offered more positively than in the bargaining stage: 'If you will agree to settle at x then I will concede y'.

- Do a deal, split the difference or bring in something new, such as extending the settlement timescale, agreeing to back-payments, phasing increases or making a joint declaration of intent to do something in the future.

- Summarize what has happened so far, emphasize the concessions that have been made and the extent of movement from the original position, and indicate that the limit has been reached.

- Apply pressure through a threat of the dire consequences that will follow if a 'final' claim is not agreed or a 'final offer' is not accepted.

Employers should not make a final offer unless they mean it. If it is not really their final offer and the union calls their bluff, they may have to make further concessions and their credibility will be undermined. Each party will attempt to force the other side into revealing the extent to which they have reached their final position. But negotiators should not allow themselves to be pressurized. They have to use their judgement on when to say 'this is as far as we can go'. That judgement will be based on their understanding that the stage when a settlement is possible has been reached.

Negotiating skills

The skills and qualities required to be effective in negotiations and bargaining are:

- *Analytical ability* – the capacity to assess the factors that affect the negotiating stance and tactics of both parties.

- *Empathy* – the ability to put oneself in the other party's shoes.

- *Interactive skills* – the ability to relate well with other people.

- *Communicating skills* – the ability to convey information and arguments clearly, positively and logically.

- *Keeping cards close to the chest* – not giving away what you really want or are prepared to concede until you are ready to do so (in the marketplace it is always easier for sellers to drive a hard bargain with buyers who have revealed somehow that they covet the article).

- *Flexible realism* – the capacity to make realistic moves during the bargaining process to reduce the claim or increase the offer, which will demonstrate that the bargainer is seeking a reasonable settlement and is prepared to respond appropriately to movements from the other side.

- *Resilience* – the ability to withstand pressure.

TIPS

- Prepare for the case by listing the arguments to be used in supporting your case and by considering the arguments or counter-arguments the other party is likely to use.

- Open the negotiation realistically and move moderately.

- Always make conditional proposals: 'If you will do this, then I will consider doing that' – the words to remember are: 'if… then …'.

- Don't give away what you really want to achieve or are prepared to concede until you are ready to do so.

- Open realistically and move moderately.

- Adopt a 'flexible realistic' approach – making realistic moves during the bargaining process.

- Never make one-sided concessions: always trade off against a concession from the other party: 'If I concede x, then I expect you to concede y'.

Leadership skills 27

People professionals need to know about leadership for four reasons: 1) they have to exercise leadership in persuading others to do things; 2) they are concerned with the development of leaders in the organization; 3) at a more senior level they have to lead teams; and 4) they are involved in leading change. The purpose of this chapter is to meet this need by analysing the process of leadership and the skills involved. It is set out under the following headings:

1 The meaning of leadership

2 Leadership theories

3 What leaders do

4 Leadership styles

5 Types of leaders

6 Effective leaders

7 The reality of leadership

8 Tips

The meaning of leadership

To lead people is to influence, guide and inspire. Leadership can be described as the ability to persuade others willingly to behave differently. It is the process of getting people to do their best to achieve a desired result. It involves developing and communicating a vision for the future. As Stogdill (1950) explained, leadership is an 'influencing process aimed at goal achievement'.

Leadership theories

Leadership is a complicated notion and a number of theories have been produced to explain it. These theories, as summarized below, have developed over the years and explore a number of different facets of leadership and leadership behaviour. In many ways they complement one another and together they help to gain a comprehensive understanding of what the process of leadership is about.

Trait theory, which explains leadership by reference to the qualities leaders have, is the basic and to many people the most familiar theory. But it has its limitations, and pragmatic research was carried out to identify what types of behaviour characterized leadership rather than focusing on the personalities of leaders. The key leadership behaviour studies conducted by the Universities of Michigan and Ohio State led to the identification of two dimensions of leadership behaviour: employee as distinct from job-centred behaviour, and the processes of consideration and initiating structure.

The next step in the development of leadership theory was the recognition by researchers that what leaders did and how they did it was dependent or contingent on the situation they were in (Fiedler, 1967). Different traits became important; different behaviours or styles of leadership had to be used to achieve effectiveness in different situations. These studies resulted in the theories of contingent and situational leadership.

Next, traits theory was in effect revived by Goleman (2001) in the notion of emotional intelligence as a necessary attribute of leaders.

The problem with leadership theories

Despite of all the research and theorizing, the concept of leadership is still problematic. As Meindl et al. (1985) commented:

> It has become apparent that, after years of trying, we have been unable to generate an understanding of leadership that is both intellectually compelling and emotionally satisfying. The concept of leadership remains elusive and enigmatic.

These problems may arise because, as a notion, leadership is difficult to pin down. There are many different types of situations in which leaders operate, many different types of leaders and many different leadership styles. Producing one theory that covers all these variables is difficult if not impossible. All that can be done is to draw on the various theories that exist to explain different facets of leadership without necessarily relying on any one of them for a comprehensive explanation of what is involved.

Perhaps leadership is best defined by considering what leaders do and how they do it (the different styles they adopt), examining what sort of leaders carry out these activities and practise these styles, and looking at any empirical evidence available on what makes them good leaders. These are all covered in the next four sections of this chapter.

What leaders do

The most convincing analysis of what leaders do was produced some time ago by John Adair (1973). He explained that the three essential roles of leaders are to:

- *Define the task* – they make it quite clear what the group is expected to do.
- *Achieve the task* – that is why the group exists. Leaders ensure that the group's purpose is fulfilled. If it is not, the result is frustration, disharmony, criticism and, eventually perhaps, disintegration of the group.
- *Maintain effective relationships* – between themselves and the members of the group, and between the people within the group. These relationships are effective if they contribute to achieving the task. They can be divided into those concerned with the team and its morale and sense of common purpose, and those concerned with individuals and how they are motivated.

Adair suggested that demands on leaders are best expressed as the ability to satisfy these three areas of need. As can be seen in Figure 27.1, he modelled these demands as three interlocking circles.

This model indicates that the task, individual and group needs are inter-dependent. Satisfying task needs will also satisfy group and individual needs. Task needs, however, cannot be met unless attention is paid to individual and group needs, and looking after individual needs will also contribute to satisfying group needs, and vice versa. There is a risk of becoming so task-oriented that leaders ignore individual and group or team needs. It is just as dangerous to be too people-oriented, focusing on meeting individual or group needs at the expense of the task. The best leaders are those who keep these three needs satisfied and in balance, according to the demands of the situation.

Figure 27.1   John Adair's model of leadership

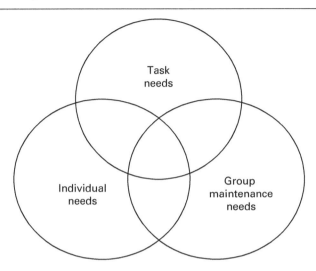

Leadership styles

Leadership style is the approach managers use in exercising leadership when they are relating to their team members. It is sometimes called 'management style'. There are many styles of leadership and no one style is necessarily better than the other in any situation. To greater or lesser degrees, leaders can be autocratic or democratic, controlling or enabling, task-oriented or people-centred. Goleman (2000) identified the following six styles and indicated when they might be used:

- *Coercive* – demands compliance (use in a crisis or with problem people).
- *Authoritative* – mobilizes people (use when new vision and direction is needed).
- *Affiliative* – creates harmony (use to heal wounds and to motivate people under stress).
- *Democratic* – forges consensus (use to build agreement and get contributions).
- *Pace-setting* – sets high standards (use to get fast results from a motivated team).
- *Coaching* – develops people (use to improve performance and develop strengths).

In line with contingency and situational theories it should not be assumed that any one style is right in any circumstances. There is no such thing as an ideal leadership style. The factors affecting the degree to which a style is appropriate will be the type of organization, the nature of the task, the characteristics of the individuals in the leader's team (the followers) and of the group as a whole and, importantly, the personality of the leader.

Effective leaders are capable of flexing their style to meet the demands of the situation. Normally democratic leaders may have to shift into more of a directive mode when faced with a crisis, but they make clear what they are doing and why. Poor leaders change their style arbitrarily so that their team members are confused and do not know what to expect next.

Good leaders may also flex their style when dealing with individual team members according to their characteristics. Some people need more positive directions than others. Others respond best if they are involved in decision making with their boss. But there is a limit to the degree of flexibility that should be used. It is unwise to differentiate too much between the ways in which individuals are treated or to be inconsistent in one's approach.

Types of leaders

To understand the process of leadership (and, incidentally, provide a basis for leadership development programmes) it is useful not only to analyse the styles that leaders can adopt but also to classify the different types of leaders that apply those styles. As described below, leaders can be charismatic, visionary, transformational, transactional or 'authentic'. However, typical leaders may exhibit any or even all of these characteristics either consistently or in response to the situation in which they find themselves.

Many studies focus on the importance of top managers as 'charismatic' or 'visionary' leaders. But leadership needs to be spread throughout the organization (distributed leadership) amongst people working together by processes of influence and interdependence. Huczynski and Buchanan (2007) commented that: 'Leadership is a widely distributed phenomenon. Leadership functions are best carried out by those who have the interest, knowledge, skills and motivation to perform them effectively.' The possibility that people who become managers may not have these qualities to a desirable extent creates a need for systematic leadership development programmes.

Charismatic leaders

Charismatic leaders rely on their personality, their inspirational qualities and their 'aura' to get people to follow them. Burns (1978) suggested that charismatic leaders were set apart from ordinary people and treated as being endowed with exceptional powers or qualities that inspire followers.

Conger and Kanungo (1998) described charismatic leadership as a process of formulating an inspiring vision of the future and then demonstrating the importance of the articulated vision. This may involve unconventional behaviour that conveys important goals that are part of the vision and demonstrates means to achieve these goals. Charismatic leaders also take risks and motivate followers by setting a personal example. In this sense, charismatic leaders operate as visionary and transformational leaders, as described below.

But Carey (1992) emphasized that:

> When the gifts of charisma, inspiration, consideration and intellectual strength are abused for the self-interest of the leader, the effect on followers ceases to be liberating and moral and becomes instead oppressive and ideological.

And Bennis (2010) commented: 'The ability to inspire trust, not charisma, is what enables leaders to recruit others to a cause.'

Visionary leaders

Visionary leaders are inspired by a clear vision of an exciting future and inspire their followers by successfully conveying that vision to them. Bennis and Nanus (1985) defined a vision as 'a target that beckons'. Their notion of visionary leadership was explained as follows:

> To choose a direction, a leader must first have developed a mental image of a possible and desirable future state of the organization. This image, which we call a vision, may be as vague as a dream or as precise as a goal or mission statement. The critical point is that a vision articulates a view of a realistic, credible and attractive future for the organization, a condition that is different in some important ways from one that now exists.

Kouzes and Posner (2003) claimed that: 'One of *the* most important practices of leadership is giving life and work a sense of meaning and purpose by offering an exciting vision.'

Transformational leaders

Transformational leaders are able, by their force of personality, to make significant changes in the behaviour of their followers in order to achieve the leader's vision or goals. As described by Burns (1978), what he called 'transforming leadership' involves motivating people to strive for higher goals. He believed that good leadership implies a moral responsibility to respond to the values and needs of people in a way that is conducive to the highest form of human relations. As he put it: 'The ultimate test of moral leadership is its capacity to transcend the claims of the multiplicity of everyday needs, wants and expectations'

Another researcher, Bass (1985), extended the work of Burns by explaining the psychological mechanisms that underlie transforming leadership. He pointed out that the extent to which leaders are transformational is measured by their influence on their followers in terms of the degree to which they feel trust, admiration, loyalty and respect for the leader and are willing to work harder than originally expected. According to Bass, this occurs because the leader transforms and motivates through an inspiring mission and vision and gives them an identity. Tichy and Devanna (1986) concluded that the transformational leader has three main roles: recognizing the need for revitalization, creating a new vision and institutionalizing change.

Yukl (1999) advised that transformational leaders should:

- develop a challenging and attractive vision together with employees;
- tie the vision to a strategy for its achievement;
- develop the vision, specify and translate it to actions;
- express confidence, decisiveness and optimism about the vision and its implementation;
- realize the vision through small, planned steps and small successes on the path to its full implementation.

Transactional leaders

Transactional leaders trade money, jobs and security for compliance. As Burns (1978) noted: 'Such leadership occurs when a person takes the initiative in making contact with others for the purpose of an exchange of valued things.' Tavanti (2008) stated that:

> Transactional leaders exhibit specific leadership skills usually associated with
> the ability to obtain results, to control through structures and processes, to solve

problems, to plan and organize, and work within the structures and boundaries of the organization.

Put like this, a transactional leader conforms to the stereotype of the manager rather than the leader. Bass (1985) argued that leaders can display both transformational and transactional characteristics. Tavanti also observed that transactional leadership behaviour is used to one degree or another by most leaders, but that:

> Particular instances of transactional leadership are motivated simply by people's wants and preferences. This form of leadership uncritically responds to our preferences, that is, even when they are grounded in base motivations or an undeveloped moral sense.

Authentic leaders

The concept of the authentic leader was originally defined by George (2003) as follows:

> Authentic leaders genuinely desire to serve others through their leadership. They are more interested in empowering the people they lead to make a difference than they are in power, money or prestige for themselves. They lead with purpose, meaning and values. They build enduring relationships with them. Others follow them because they know where they stand. They are consistent and self-disciplined.

Authenticity was described by Harter (2002) as 'owning one's personal experiences, be they thoughts, emotions, needs, preferences, or beliefs, processes captured by the injunction to know oneself and behaving in accordance with the true self'. Authentic leadership is based on a positive moral perspective characterized by high ethical standards that guide decision making and behaviour (May et al., 2003). As Avolio et al. (2004) explained, authentic leaders act in accordance with deep personal values and convictions to build credibility and win the respect and trust of followers. By encouraging diverse viewpoints and building networks of collaborative relationships with followers, they lead in a manner that followers perceive and describe as *authentic*.

George et al. (2007) set out the basis of authentic leadership as follows:

> We all have the capacity to inspire and empower others. But we must first be willing to devote ourselves to our personal growth and development as leaders... No one can be authentic by trying to imitate someone else. You can

learn from others' experiences, but there is no way you can be successful when you are trying to be like them. People trust you when you are genuine and authentic, not a replica of someone else.

Authentic leadership is, in essence, ethical leadership. Walumbwa et al. (2008) claimed that it can lead to enhanced trust, job satisfaction and performance.

Leadership skills

Effective leaders are confident and know where they want to go and what they want to do. They have the ability to take charge, convey their vision to their team, get their team members into action and ensure that they achieve their agreed goals. They know how to build well-functioning teams. They are trustworthy, good at influencing people and earn the respect of their team. They are aware of their own strengths and weaknesses and are skilled at understanding what will motivate their team members. They appreciate the advantages of consulting and involving people in decision making. They can switch flexibly from one leadership style to another to meet the demands of different situations and people.

It is generally accepted that one of the key skills a leader or manager needs is an ability to analyse and read situations and establish order and clarity in situations of ambiguity. Gold et al. (2010) stated that: 'Leadership demands a sense of purpose, and an ability to influence others, interpret situations, negotiate and express their views, often in the face of opposition.'

Brindle (2016) reported research commissioned by Firstline, the social work training organization. The finding of the study, which obtained evidence from 169 key figures in the social work sector, was that outstanding leaders create a climate that energizes teams to improve the impact they make, giving them stability, clear direction and definition of role, plus the space and time to reflect on practice and develop their own leadership skills.

Effective leaders endeavour to answer the following questions about the individuals in the group and the team.

Individuals

The questions leaders need to answer about their individual team members are:

- What are their strengths and weaknesses?

- What are their needs, attitudes, perspectives and preferences?
- What are likely to be the best ways of motivating them?
- What tasks are they best at doing?
- Is there scope to increase flexibility by developing new skills?
- How well do they perform in achieving targets and performance standards?
- To what extent can they manage their own performance and development?
- Are there any areas where there is a need to develop skill or competence?
- How can I provide them with the sort of support and guidance that will improve their performance?
- What can be done to improve the performance of any individuals in the group by coaching or mentoring?

The team

The questions leaders need to answer about their team are:

- How well is the team organized?
- Is the team clear about what is expected of it?
- Do the members of the team work well together?
- If there is any conflict between team members, how can I resolve it?
- How can the commitment and motivation of the team be achieved?
- Are team members flexible – capable of carrying out different tasks?
- To what extent can the team manage its own performance?
- Is there scope to empower the team so that it can take on greater responsibility for setting standards, monitoring performance and taking corrective action?
- Can the team be encouraged to work together to produce ideas for improving performance?
- What is the team good and not so good at doing?
- What can I do to improve the performance of the team through coaching and mentoring?

The reality of leadership

The reality of leadership is that many first-line managers and team leaders are appointed or promoted to their posts with some idea, possibly, of what their managerial or supervisory duties are, but with no appreciation of the leadership skills they need. They see their role as being to tell people what to do and then see that they do it. They may tend to adopt a transactional approach, focusing on getting the job done and neglecting everything else. They may not be charismatic, visionary or transformational leaders because even if they have the latent qualities required, their situation does not seem to require or encourage any of these approaches.

However, the better ones will rely on their know-how (authority goes to the person who knows), their quiet confidence and their cool, analytical approach to dealing with problems. Any newly appointed leader or individual who is progressing to a higher level of leadership will benefit from a leadership development programme which will help them to understand and apply the skills they need.

TIPS

- Examine the various explanations of the qualities that make a good leader and use them to assess the levels of leadership achieved in your organization and what needs to be done to make any improvements required.

- Assess your own strengths and weaknesses as a leader by reference to the qualities.

- Think about or observe any managers you know whom you have worked for or with and consider what you can learn from them about effective and less effective leadership behaviours.

- Examine the various explanations of the qualities that make a good leader and use them to assess the levels of leadership achieved in your organization and any improvements required.

References

Adair, J (1973) *The Action-centred Leader*, London, McGraw-Hill

Avolio, B J, Gardner, W L, Walumbwa, F O, Luthans, F and May, D R (2004) Unlocking the mask: A look at the process by which authentic leaders impact follower attitudes and behaviours, *Leadership Quarterly*, **15**, pp 801–23

Bass, B M (1985) *Leadership and Performance*, New York, Free Press

Bennis, W (2010) We need leaders, *Leadership Excellence*, **27** (12), p 4

Bennis, W and Nanus, B (1985) *Leadership: The strategies for taking charge*, New York, Harper & Row

Brindle, D (2016), Leadership, *The Guardian: Social work on the front line*, 16 March, pp 8–9

Burns, J M (1978) *Leadership*, New York, Harper & Row

Carey, M R (1992) Transformational leadership and the fundamental option for self-transcendence, *Leadership Quarterly*, **3**, pp 217–36

Conger, J A and Kanungo, R N (1998) *Charismatic Leadership in Organizations*, Thousand Oaks, CA, Sage

Fiedler, F E (1967) *A Theory of Leadership Effectiveness*, New York, McGraw-Hill

George, B (2003) *Authentic Leadership*, San Francisco, CA, Jossey-Bass

George, B, Sims, P, McLean, A N and Mayer, D (2007) Discovering your authentic leadership, *Harvard Business Review*, February, pp 129–38

Gold, J, Thorpe, R and Mumford, A (2010) *Gower Handbook of Leadership and Management Development*, Farnham, Gower

Goleman, D (2000) Leadership that gets results, *Harvard Business Review*, March–April, pp 78–90

Goleman, D (2001) *What Makes a Leader*, Boston, MA, Harvard Business School Press

Harter, S (2002) Authenticity, in (eds) C R Snyder and S J Lopez, *Handbook of Positive Psychology*, Oxford, Oxford University Press, pp 382–94

Huczynski, A A and Buchanan, D A (2007) *Organizational Behaviour*, 6th edn, Harlow, FT Prentice Hall

Kouzes, J and Posner, B (2003) *The Leadership Challenge*, San Francisco, CA, Jossey-Bass

May, D R, Chan, A, Hodges, T and Avolio, B J (2003) Developing the moral component of authentic leadership, *Organizational Dynamics*, **32** (3), pp 247–60

Meindl, J R, Ehrlich, S B and Dukerich, J M (1985) The romance of leadership, *Administrative Science Quarterly*, **30** (1), pp 78–102

Stogdill, R M (1950) Leaders, membership and organization, *Psychological Bulletin*, **25**, pp 1–14

Tavanti, M (2008) Transactional leadership, in (eds) A Marturano and J Gosling, *Leadership: The key concepts*, London, Routledge, pp 166–70

Tichy, N M and Devanna, M A (1986) *The Transformational Leader*, New York, Wiley

Walumbwa, F O, Avolio, B J, Gardner, W L, Wernsing, T S and Peterson, S J (2008) Authentic leadership: development and validation of a theory-based measure, *Journal of Management*, **34** (1), pp 89–126

Yukl, G (1999) An evaluation of conceptual weaknesses in transformational and charismatic leadership theories, *Leadership Quarterly*, **10**, pp 285–305

Consultancy skills   28

People management professionals spend much of their time on a day-to-day basis advising senior managers and line managers on what should be done to deal with people management requirements and issues and solve people problems. When doing this they are in effect acting as consultants, albeit informally. They can also be involved in running or taking part in more formal assignments in order to develop new or substantially revised people management strategies, policies and practices thus taking on the role of internal consultant. This chapter is set out under the following headings:

1 Consultancy activities

2 Consultancy skills

3 Tips

Consultancy activities

The main areas that could be covered in a formal consultancy project are:

- *Strategic studies* – the development of broad people strategies and policies.
- *Process consulting* – the provision of advice and help using organizational development techniques in process areas such as organization, quality management, performance management, team building, conflict resolution and change management.
- *Problem solving* – providing solutions to organizational and management problems.
- *Systems development* – the introduction or amendment of people management systems and procedures.

The stages of a formal consultancy project are:

- *Identification.* The reasons for the projected consultancy exercise are established and the relevant facts about the circumstances and requirements assembled. This leads to a definition of the purpose of the project or assignment and its terms of reference.

- *Project planning.* Decisions are made on what work needs to be done, who does it, the timetable, the financial budget, and methods of monitoring and controlling progress.

- *Data collection.* Information is assembled on present arrangements and any issues and problems that need to be dealt with. The aim is to ensure that any decisions will be evidence-based.

- *Analysis.* The data and evidence that has been gathered is subjected to systematic examination so that it can be resolved into its key elements and logical patterns, thus promoting understanding and pointing the way to an appropriate diagnosis. Opinions will be subjected to critical analysis to find out the extent to which they are founded on fact.

- *Diagnosis.* The real needs of the organization or the root cause or causes of the problem (not the symptoms) are identified. A good diagnosis will be based on rigorous analysis and will establish not only the immediate factors to be taken into account but the longer-term implications. It will avoid simplistic explanations. So far as possible the diagnosis is specific but it might be necessary to present a general picture of the context in which the situation has arisen that has prompted the need for action.

- *Conclusions and recommendations.* These flow logically from the analysis and diagnosis. They spell out what should be done, why it should be done and the costs and benefits of doing it (a cost-benefit analysis) There will inevitably be alternative solutions or courses of action that will have to be evaluated. The recommendation indicates how they will be implanted, the timetable for implementation and the resources required.

Consultancy skills

Consultants need process, analytical, interpersonal, communication and project management skills.

- *Process skills.* Building trusting relationships with the people involved in the assignment in order to diagnose the underlying causes of issues and help them to recognize these and develop and own their own solutions

The originator of process consulting Ed Schein (Brendel, 2023) related in his final piece of work on 'humble consulting' that while 'we sometimes become caught up in our desire to develop competency models and new pedagogies and toolkits, we must recognize that effective solutions rarely live in thick binders full of data and instead, consultants need the ability to step back, to always be curious, empathetic and helpful and always know what is going on within the organization before giving advice. [They need to] get the whole picture – ask: "How did we get here?"'

- *Analytical skills*. These enable insight to be obtained on relevant issues They involve the ability to visualize, articulate and solve complex problems and concepts and make decisions based on available information. Problem-solving techniques are used. The skills required include the capacity to evaluate that information to assess its significance, and the ability to apply logical and critical thinking to the situation. Analytical skills involve considering a complex situation and breaking it down to its constituent but inter-related parts in order to understand it.

- *Interpersonal skills*. Consultancy assignments may involve a lot of grappling with facts but they are essentially dominated and governed by the relationships between the people involved and the level of interpersonal skills that are used. Consultants need the ability to interact with people effectively. They need to be persuasive – good at case presentation – making and presenting a convincing evidence-based business case for their proposals. They need generally to be good communicators as described below.

- *Communication skills*. Consultants usually have to present written findings and recommendations in writing and report-writing skills are therefore required. They may additionally be expected to present their findings orally and therefore need presentation skills.

- *Project management skills*. Project management skills are needed to plan, operate and control assignment programmes to ensure that the specified outcomes are delivered on time.

TIPS

- Identify and define the real issue or problem.
- Decide on the results required and how these results will be measured. Explore alternative ways of conducting the project.

- Define specific terms of reference and deliverables.
- Draw up an assignment programme with progress review dates for agreed deliverables. Monitor progress accordingly.
- Be prepared to modify the terms of reference if new circumstances arise.
- Evaluate recommendations on the basis of the degree to which they meet objectives, the ease of implementation, their costs, the benefits arising from them and their acceptability to stakeholders.
- Draw up and put into effect an implementation programme involving those affected as much as possible.

Reference

Brendel, W (2023) 'A Most Sacred Fireside', OpenSourceOD Blog, January 28, https://www.opensourceod.com/post/a-most-sacred-fireside-ed-schein-s-final-evening-with-the-od-community (archived at https://perma.cc/YT6D-KRWM)

PART FIVE
People skills

Handling people problems

29

Handling people problems is an important part of the people professional's role, either advising line managers on what they should do about a problem or dealing with a problem directly, for example when a disciplinary procedure case has to be dealt with. The chapter starts with general discussions on the characteristics of people problems and how they should be dealt with. These are followed by descriptions of the approaches that can be adopted to deal with particular cases. The chapter is set out under the following headings:

1 The nature of people problems

2 Ways of handling people problems

3 Conducting a disciplinary meeting

4 Dealing with negative behaviour

5 Dealing with under-performance

6 Dealing with absenteeism

7 Dealing with poor timekeeping

8 Handling complaints and grievances

9 Tips

The nature of people problems

People problems may arise from issues concerning discipline, performance, complaints and grievances, and conflict.

Discipline

Discipline is the regulation of the activities of people at work in order to obtain compliance to standards of behaviour or to work requirements.

Disciplinary action may be taken to deal with misconduct, for example bullying, harassment, insubordination or absence without leave. When serious misconduct occurs such as theft, fraud, physical violence or gross negligence, it may be called gross misconduct and lead to instant dismissal.

Line managers and supervisors exert discipline on a day-to-day basis which, depending on the situation and the people involved, can be lightweight or, to various degrees, oppressive. Unwritten behavioural or cultural norms may define what is regarded as appropriate behaviour. In addition, there may be written rules or regulations defining expected behaviour which are incorporated in a disciplinary procedure that sets out the stages through which disciplinary actions should proceed. These start with an informal discussion and, if the behaviour does not improve, continue with the increasingly severe actions of an informal warning, a written warning and, finally, if the procedure has been exhausted, disciplinary action.

Line managers and supervisors are responsible for maintaining discipline but they will benefit from support, guidance and training from people professionals. The latter may get involved in disciplinary interviews in the later stages of a disciplinary procedure to provide advice to the manager and ensure that the procedure is being followed properly. They may also hear appeals.

Performance

Poor performance can be the fault of the individual, in which case remedial action is necessary. But it could arise because of inadequate training, poor leadership or problems in the system of work.

Complaints and grievances

The words complaint and grievance are often used interchangeably but there is a difference. A complaint is the expression of dissatisfaction by someone about the way they are being treated or their working conditions. A grievance is a complaint that has been presented to management to be dealt with formally using a grievance procedure.

Conflict

Conflict involves disagreement or controversy. It is the struggle or clash between opposing forces taking the form of a state of opposition between ideas and interests. It can occur between individuals, between groups within the organization, e.g. different departments, and between employees and their employer over terms and conditions of employment. Methods of tackling conflict are discussed in Chapter 32.

Ways of handling people problems

The four fundamental ways to handle problems are to treat people with respect, empathize with them, adopt a problem-solving approach and use the right tone.

Treat people with respect

To respect someone is to recognize a person's qualities, to ensure that they feel valued and treat them with dignity and courtesy – no belittling, no bullying. It means being sensitive to the differences between people, taking this diversity into account in any dealings with them. It involves honouring their contribution and listening to what they have to say. It means recognizing that people may have legitimate grievances and responding to them promptly, fully and sympathetically. Importantly, it recognizes that the purpose of any meeting between an individual and their manager or a people professional is to identify and resolve a problem. Meetings should be used to explore all the factors surrounding a situation. They should not be vehicles for blame or criticism.

Alison Green (2019) advised that when dealing with people problems:

> The kindest thing you can do is to be really clear with people… Talk, don't scold. Often all you need to do is to make the point that you are concerned about something by simply talking over what happened, why it happened and how to avoid the problem in the future.

Empathizing

Empathizing with people means getting to know their point of view: where they are coming from, how they see the situation they are in, what they would like to do, how they want to be treated. It means that you have to listen to them carefully, ask questions to ensure that you understand their situation and, as necessary, adjust your views to accommodate what you have learnt.

Problem solving

To address an issue a problem-solving approach is required. This means that you and/or the line manager involved in conjunction with the employee:

1 Get the facts. Make sure that you have all the information or evidence you need to understand exactly what the problem is. People should only be judged on the basis of the facts, not on opinions about the facts.

2 Weigh and decide. Analyse the facts to identify the causes of the problem. Consider any alternative solutions to the problem and decide which is likely to be the most successful.

3 Take action. Following the decision, plan what is to be done, establish goals and success criteria and put the plan into effect.

4 Check results. Monitor the implementation of the plan and check that the expected results have been obtained.

Tone

When you are conducting a meeting with an employee to address an issue such as poor performance or alleged unacceptable behaviour, e.g. bullying, how you talk to the person and your manner – your tone – are important.

Alison Green (2019) observed that: 'Your tone matters... a lot. Be clear and distinct when dealing with a problem but your tone can still be kind and compassionate.'

The tone you adopt should be appropriate to the situation. When the problem is a personal one, you should be sympathetic and compassionate. When you are dealing with a performance issue, your tone should be understanding, conveying that you appreciate what is involved and have taken on board the individual's point of view. This can be done by reflecting the individual's remarks, saying something like: 'I gather from what you have just said that...'. If the problem is a serious behavioural one, you can adopt a more neutral but not unfriendly tone. But in these circumstances you should avoid any hostile, disapproving tone of voice. Don't criticize or attach blame. Your job is to get the facts and come to a conclusion on what needs to be done about them. A premature expression of opinion, even if it is conveyed simply by a tone or voice or manner, offends a principle of natural justice – that people should only be judged on the basis of the facts, not on opinions about the facts. Moreover, it will prejudice a full and fair review of the issue and inhibit the right of the employee to get a fair hearing.

Conducting a disciplinary meeting

A disciplinary meeting is conducted in five steps.

1 Preparation

Establish what the issue is. Get all the facts, including witness statements. Ensure that you get as full a picture as possible. Consider how these facts may be interpreted by the parties involved. Obtain basic details about the employee. Decide how you are going to conduct the meeting and how the evidence should be presented. Invite the employee to the meeting in writing, explaining why it is being held and that he or she has the right to have someone present at the meeting on his or her behalf.

2 Opening

Start the meeting by explaining why it is taking place, stating what the issue is and spelling out the facts of the situation rather than any managerial feelings of annoyance about them. Discipline starts from management dissatisfaction, so the opening move is for you to explain why such dissatisfaction exists. As Derek Torrington (2013) pointed out, 'This shows that you see the interview as a way of dealing with a problem of the working situation and not (at least not yet) as a way of dealing with an unsatisfactory employee'. Torrington also observed that:

> Disciplinary situations are at least disconcerting for employees and frequently very worrying, surrounded by feelings of hostility and mistrust, so that it is to be expected that some ill-feeling will be pent up and waiting for the opportunity to be vented... It is almost inevitable that the interviewee will start the interview defensively, expecting to be blamed for something and therefore ready to refute any allegations, probably deflecting blame elsewhere. The manager needs to anticipate the respondent's initial reaction and be prepared to deal with the reaction as well as the facts that have already been collected.

3 Discussion

The meeting should continue by getting the employee to explain the facts giving their reasons for their behaviour. The aim is to ensure that you are aware of the background to the problem and the employee has the opportunity to present their own version of the facts, perhaps challenging those you have presented on behalf of management. Give the employee plenty of time to respond and state their case. Take a break as required to consider the points raised and to relieve any pressure in the meeting.

Where versions differ, which they may well do as the employee is probably on the defensive, you have to judge which version is more likely to be correct. If you are certain that the facts as assembled by you are correct, you can go on to the next step having explained why. But if the information is uncertain you may have to adjourn the meeting in order to re-examine the situation. If this review confirms management's version that there is a disciplinary case, you can reconvene the meeting.

4 Decision

Once the facts have been established and as far as possible accepted or confirmed, the outcome may simply be an agreement on what the employee needs to do to improve without any disciplinary action. But following the first stage of a disciplinary procedure, in more serious cases an informal, i.e. unwritten, warning may be given that unless improvement is made in some specified way a formal written warning will be given. If the same situation arises at the next stage the written warning may state that severe disciplinary action may be taken if the behaviour persists. The ultimate decision may be dismissal or some other penalty such as suspension.

5 Closure

The closure should be as positive as possible so that those concerned put the procedure behind them. As Torrington points out: 'It can never be appropriate to close an interview leaving the employee humbled and demotivated'.

Dealing with negative behaviour

Negative behaviour may take the form of lack of interest in the work, unwillingness to cooperate with team leaders or other members of the team, making unjustified complaints about the work or working conditions, grumbling at being asked to carry out a perfectly reasonable task, objecting strongly to being asked to do something extra (or even refusing to do it) – 'It's not in my job description' – or, in extreme cases, insolence.

People exhibiting negative behaviour may be quietly resentful rather than openly disruptive. They mutter away in the background at meetings and lack enthusiasm.

A certain amount of negative behaviour can be tolerated as long as the individual works reasonably well and does not upset other team members. They have simply to say to themselves, 'It takes all sorts…' and put up with it, although a manager might calmly say during a review meeting, 'You're doing a good job but…'. If, however, they take this line they have to be specific. They must cite actual instances. It is no good making generalized accusations that will either be openly refuted or internalized by the receiver, making him or her even more resentful.

If the negative behaviour means that the individual's contribution is not acceptable and is disruptive, action has to be taken. Negative people can be quiet but they are usually angry about something; their negative behaviour is an easy way of expressing their anger. To deal with the problem it is necessary to find out what has made them angry.

Causes of negative behaviour

There are many possible causes of negative behaviour, which could include one or more of the following:

- a real or imagined slight from their manager or a colleague;
- a feeling of being put upon;
- a belief that the contribution they make is neither appreciated nor rewarded properly in terms of pay or promotion;
- resentment at what was perceived to be unfair criticism;
- anger directed at the company or their manager because what was considered to be a reasonable request (such as for leave or a transfer) was turned down, or because of an unfair accusation.

Dealing with the problem

It is because there can be such a variety of real or imagined causes of negative behaviour that dealing with it becomes one of the most difficult tasks line managers and people professionals have to undertake. If the action taken is crude or insensitive the negative behaviour will only be intensified. This might mean having to invoke the disciplinary procedure, which should be a last resort.

In one sense, it is easier to deal with an actual example of negative behaviour. This can be handled on the spot. If the problem is one of general attitude rather than specific actions it is more difficult to cope with. Hard evidence may not be available. When individuals are accused of being, for example, generally unenthusiastic or uncooperative, they can simply go into denial and accuse you of being prejudiced. Their negative behaviour may be reinforced.

It is best to deal with this sort of problem informally, either when it arises or at any point during the year when it is felt that something has to be done about it. An annual formal performance review or appraisal meeting is not the right time, especially if it produces ratings that are linked to a pay increase. Raising the issue then will only put individuals on the defensive and a productive discussion will be impossible.

The discussion may be informal but it should have three clear objectives:

1 To review the situation with individuals, the aim being if possible to get them to recognize for themselves that they are behaving negatively. If this cannot be achieved, then the objective is to bring to the attention of individuals your belief that their behaviour is unacceptable in certain ways.

2 To establish the reasons for the individuals' negative behaviour so far as this is feasible.

3 To agree any actions individuals could take to behave more positively, or what you or the organization could do to remove the causes of the behaviour.

Discussing the problem

The starting point should be general questions about how individuals feel about their work. Do they have any problems in carrying it out? Are they happy with the support they get from you or their colleagues? Are they satisfied that they are pulling their weight to the best of their ability?

This generalized start provides the basis for the next two stages – identifying causes and any remedies. It is best if individuals are encouraged to decide for themselves that there is a problem, but in many, if not the majority of cases, this is unlikely to happen. Individuals may not recognize that they are behaving negatively or will not be prepared to admit it.

It is then necessary to discuss the problem. They should be given time to say their piece. The response should spell out how justifiable grievances will be dealt with or why no action is necessary. In the latter case, an explanation should be given as to why the individual's behaviour gives the impression of being negative. This should be specific, bringing up actual instances. For example, a discussion could be based on the following questions: 'Do you recall yesterday's team meeting?', 'How did you think it went?', 'How helpful do you think you were in dealing with the problem?', 'Do you remember saying… ?', 'How helpful do you think that remark was?', 'Would it surprise you to learn that I felt you had not been particularly helpful in the following ways… ?'

Of course, even if this careful approach is adopted, individuals may still refuse to admit that there is anything wrong with their behaviour. If this impasse is reached, then there is no alternative but to spell out where it is believed they have gone wrong. But this should be done in a positive way: 'Then I think that it is only fair for me to point out to you that your contribution (to the meeting) would have been more helpful if you had…'.

Establishing the cause or causes

If the negative behaviour is because of a real or imagined grievance about what the manager, colleagues or the organization have done, then the individual has to be persuaded to spell this out as precisely as possible. At this point, the job of the manager or HR practitioner is to listen, not to judge. People can be just as angry about imaginary as real slights. You have to find out how they perceive the problem before you can deal with it.

It may emerge during the discussion that the problem has nothing to do with the manager or the company. It may be family troubles or worries about health or finance. If this is the case a sympathetic approach is appropriate, which may involve suggesting remedies in the form of counselling or practical advice from within or outside the organization. If the perceived problem is the manager, colleagues or the organization, try to get chapter and verse on what it is so that remedial action can be taken.

Taking remedial action

If the problem rests with the individual, the objective is, of course, to get them to recognize for themselves that corrective action is necessary and what they need to do about it – with help as necessary. In some situations you might suggest counselling or a source of advice might be recommended. But care needs to be taken: there should be no implication that there is something wrong with them. It is best to go no further than suggesting that individuals may find this helpful – they don't *need* it but they could *benefit* from it. Managers or HR specialists should not offer counselling themselves. This is better done by professional counsellors.

If there is anything specific that the parties involved in the situation can do, then the line to take is that the problem can be tackled together: 'This is what I will do', 'This is what the company will do', 'What do you think you should do?' If there is no response to the last question, this is the point where it is necessary to spell out the necessary action. This should be as specific as possible and expressed as suggestions, not commands. A joint problem-solving approach is always best.

Dealing with under-performance

Poor performance can be the fault of the individual but it could arise because of poor leadership or problems in the system of work. In the case of an individual, the reason may be that he or she:

- could not do it – ability;
- did not know how to do it – skill;
- would not do it – attitude; or
- did not fully understand what was expected of him or her.

Inadequate leadership from managers can be the cause of poor performance from individuals. It is the manager's responsibility to specify the results expected and the levels of skill and competence required. As likely as not, when people do not understand what they have to do, it is their manager who is to blame. And if they do not have the skills required it is possible that they have not been provided with adequate experience, guidance or training.

Performance can also be affected by the system of work. If this is badly planned and organized or does not function well, individuals cannot be blamed for the poor performance that results. This is the fault of management and they must put it right.

If inadequate individual performance cannot be attributed to poor leadership or the system of work, there are seven steps that can be taken to deal with it:

1 Identify the areas of under-performance – be specific.

2 Establish the causes of poor performance.

3 Agree on the action required.

4 Ensure that the necessary support (coaching, training, extra resources etc.) is provided to ensure the action is successful.

5 Monitor progress and provide feedback.

6 Provide additional guidance as required.

7 Consider moving the employee to a more suitable job.

8 As a last resort, invoke the capability or disciplinary procedure, starting with an informal warning.

Dealing with absenteeism

A frequent people problem managers and people professionals have to face is absenteeism. It may be necessary to deal with recurrent short-term (one or two days) absence or longer-term sickness absence.

Recurrent short-term absence

Dealing with people who are repeatedly absent for short periods can be difficult. This is because it may be hard to determine when occasional absence becomes a problem or whether it is justifiable, perhaps on medical grounds.

So what can be done about it? Many organizations provide guidelines to managers on the 'trigger points' for action (the amount of absence that needs to be investigated), perhaps based on analyses of the incidence of short-term absence and the level at which it is regarded as acceptable (there may be software to generate analyses and data that can be made available direct to managers through a self-service system). If guidelines do not exist, HR specialists should be available to provide advice.

It is necessary to decide when something needs to be done and then what to do about it. A day off every other month may not be too serious, although if it happens regularly on a Monday (after weekends in Prague, Barcelona, etc.?) or a Friday (before such weekends?) you may feel like having a word with the individual, not as a warning but just to let him or her know that you are aware of what is going on. There may be a medical or other acceptable explanation. Return-to-work interviews can provide valuable information and an opportunity to discuss any problems. The individual is seen and given the chance to explain the absence.

In persistent cases of absenteeism an absence review meeting can be held. Although this would be more comprehensive than a return-to-work interview it should not at this stage be presented as part of a disciplinary process. The meeting should be positive and constructive. If absence results from a health problem it can be established what is being done about it, and if necessary suggest that his or her doctor should be consulted. Or absences may be caused by problems facing a parent or a carer. In such cases it is right to be sympathetic but it would be reasonable to discuss with the individual what steps can be taken to reduce the problem or whether flexible working could be arranged. The aim is to get the employee to discuss as openly as possible any factors affecting his or her attendance and to agree any constructive steps.

If after holding an attendance review meeting and, it is to be hoped, agreeing the steps necessary to reduce absenteeism, short-term absence persists without a satisfactory explanation, then another meeting can be held that emphasizes the employee's responsibility for attending work. Depending on the circumstances (each case should be dealt with on its merits), at this meeting it can be indicated that absence levels should improve over a defined timescale (an improvement period). If this does not happen, the individual can expect more formal disciplinary action.

Dealing with long-term absence

Dealing with long-term absence can also be difficult. The aim should be to facilitate the employee's return to work at the earliest reasonable point while recognizing that in extreme cases the person may not be able to come back. In that case he or she can fairly be dismissed for lack of capability as long as:

- the employee has been consulted at all stages;
- contact has been maintained with the employee – this is something you can usefully do as long as you do not appear to be pressing him or her to return to work before he or she is ready;
- appropriate medical advice has been sought from the employee's own doctor, but the employee's consent is needed and employees have the right to see the report – it may be desirable to obtain a second opinion;
- all reasonable options for alternative employment have been reviewed as well as any other means of facilitating a return to work.

The decision to dismiss should only be taken if these conditions are satisfied. It is a tricky one and it may be advisable to seek advice from an employment law expert.

Dealing with poor timekeeping

A poor timekeeping record may initially be dealt with by an informal warning. But if in spite of the warning lateness persists it may be necessary to invoke the disciplinary procedure. This would go through the successive stages of a recorded oral warning, and a final written warning which would indicate that timekeeping must improve by a certain date (the improvement period) otherwise disciplinary action would take place. If the final warning does not work, such action would be taken; in serious cases this would mean dismissal.

Note that this raises the difficult question of time limits which may be given with a final warning. If timekeeping does improve by that date, and the slate is wiped clean, it might be assumed that the disciplinary procedure starts again from scratch if timekeeping deteriorates again. But it is in the nature of things that some people cannot sustain efforts to get to work on time for long, and deterioration can occur. In these circumstances, is it necessary to keep on going through the warning cycles time after time? The answer is no, and the best deal with this is to avoid stating a finite end date to a final warning period that implies a 'wipe the slate clean' approach. Instead, the warning should simply say that timekeeping performance will be reviewed on a stated date. If it has not improved, disciplinary action can be taken. If it has, no action will be taken, but the employee is warned that further deterioration will make him or her liable to disciplinary action, which may well speed up the normal procedure, perhaps by only using the final warning stage and by reducing the elapsed time between the warning and the review date. There will come a time, if poor timekeeping persists, when you can say 'enough is enough' and initiate disciplinary action.

Handling complaints and grievances

An important responsibility of people professionals is to see that complaints are handled swiftly and competently. They will advise line managers on how to deal with complaints, emphasizing that they have to be taken seriously even if they appear to be trivial. People professionals themselves will have to handle complaints when individuals are unwilling to raise them with their line manager, for example if the complaint is about the latter's behaviour. Clearly complaints involving line managers have to be resolved with them and although a discussion between individuals and people professionals must remain confidential the former must be told that it can only be dealt with if it is referred to the line manager or, in exceptional circumstances, the line manager's manager. The people professional will then ensure that the line manager treats the complaint seriously so that it doesn't become a grievance and, as necessary, advise the line manager on what should be done.

Organizations should have a grievance policy which will state that employees have the right to raise their grievances with their manager, to be accompanied by a representative if they so wish, and to appeal to a higher level if they feel that their grievance has not been resolved satisfactorily.

Dealing with complaints and grievances may mean conducting a challenging interview with an employee, as discussed in the next chapter.

TIPS

- Try your best to discuss and resolve the problem informally. Only resort to a disciplinary, capability or grievance procedure if all else fails.
- When discussing a problem with an employee use the occasion to get the facts and, if possible, reach a conclusion on how it can be resolved to the satisfaction of all concerned.
- Avoid blaming or criticizing people when discussing a problem. It will inhibit the discussion and could in any case prove to be premature when the facts of the situation are fully revealed.
- Allow a reasonable amount of scope for people to have their say but keep the meeting under control – don't permit abusive behaviour.
- *Listen* to what people have to say.
- Ensure that any action proposed is consistent with what has been done before in similar circumstances.
- Bear in mind the risk of an expensive and time-consuming unfair dismissal case if the disciplinary procedure is not followed properly.
- Allow for the fact that in a disciplinary meeting employees are likely to be on the defensive.
- Don't allow prejudices or preconceived ideas to cloud your judgement.

References

Green, A (2019) *Ask a Manager,* Piatkus

Torrington, D (2013) *Managing to Manage,* London, Kogan Page

Handling challenging conversations

A challenging conversation is one that is difficult to handle because it is about an emotional or sensitive issue – especially a personal one – or involves persuading someone to do or accept something that they don't agree with or are unhappy about. This chapter examines how to handle such conversations under the following headings:

1 The nature of challenging conversations

2 Approach to handling a challenging conversation

3 Tips for meetings to discuss problems

4 Tips for meetings to convey bad news

The nature of challenging conversations

Challenging conversations are ones in which emotions, feelings and reactions have to be managed in a sensitive way. They occur when the subject matter is contentious or sensitive or presents a personal threat, real or perceived, to either of the parties involved. They may elicit strong, complex emotions that can be hard to predict or control. Challenging conversations may arise when it is necessary to:

- investigate a complaint;
- deal with a grievance;
- comfort or reassure someone – for example, if they are to be made redundant;
- tackle a personality clash;

- deal with potentially delicate situations, such as turning down requests for annual leave or to work flexibly;
- give people bad news, for example redundancy, demotion, a negative performance appraisal, reduction in pay, failure to be promoted.

They may also occur when there's lack of clarity or confusion – for example around expectations or roles – or differences in beliefs, opinions or approaches. Negative reactions are more likely when people feel personally judged or criticized.

Many of these situations will be dealt with in the first place by line managers who may therefore benefit from training and guidance on how to handle them. This can be provided by people professionals. The latter may have challenging conversations with their line management colleagues when they are questioning the latter's behaviour in some aspect of their people management responsibilities, e.g. controlling bullying.

Line managers, and indeed people management specialists, can find it difficult to have conversations or hold meetings with individuals about performance or discipline issues. In advance these can look difficult and in practice they *can* be challenging if the manager wants to achieve desired changes or improvements in performance. They can be even more challenging in prospect if it is feared that unpleasantness can occur in the shape of lack of cooperation or outright hostility, or when this happens in spite of efforts to prevent it.

The conversation may feel particularly difficult if you need to cover a sensitive subject, need to deliver bad news or receive or give feedback, and if you're not sure how the other person (or people) in the conversation will react.

Instigating a potentially difficult conversation can feel daunting and there is a natural tendency for managers to delay taking action in the hopes that the issue will be resolved without their intervention. But this is rarely the case. Procrastination won't make problems disappear and in fact, if issues are ignored, they are likely to escalate and become even more difficult to resolve, with negative consequences. It is far better to tackle problems at an early stage as this can help to nip problems in the bud, prevent the situation from deteriorating and maintain good working relationships with colleagues.

We all tend to put off difficult conversations because of the intensity and complexity of the emotions they arouse – both for the manager who may be initiating the conversation and for the person with whom they are holding it. Fear of how people will react and whether you will be able to handle their reactions, feelings of vulnerability or concern about a loss of control can make us all reluctant to raise an issue face-to-face. You may even be concerned that you will not be supported by senior managers, or other colleagues, if you take steps to address sensitive issues. However, by adopting the right approach, preparing yourself carefully and developing the right skills, mindset and behaviour, you will be able to maximize your ability to handle the conversation effectively and steer it to a successful conclusion acceptable to all involved.

Approach to handling a challenging conversation

It's worth trying to explore the issue informally before holding a formal meeting. Consider the following aspects or steps to help you conduct it.

1 Prepare for the conversation

Approach the situation as objectively as possible. Identify the outcome you would like to achieve through the conversation. Think about what your thoughts or feelings are about the issue and how they might be affecting you. Challenge your own assumptions and beliefs. Your mindset will have a big impact on even an informal conversation. Get ready to be curious and think about what might be going on for the other person.

2 Plan the conversation

Plan to have it in a private and comfortable situation when you're both likely to be at your best and allow time for it.

Reflect on what you want to say. Consider how the other person is likely to hear it. Ask yourself two questions: 'What do I believe is the problem?' and 'What do I believe the other person thinks is the problem?' Avoid planning to say anything that could sound judgemental. Try to replace critical comments with neutral observations referring to factual information about the situation being discussed. Prepare your opening sentences, possibly writing them down.

3 Carry out the conversation

During the conversation listen carefully to what the other person has to say. Try and understand where they are coming from. Be open to the other person's perspective. Show empathy by reflecting back the things that you hear. Stick to the facts. If you are discussing a contentious issue, present your side of the story and listen to their side of the story. If the conversation is becoming tense, slow it down or pause it.

4 Reach a conclusion

Be future-focused. Once you have listened to each other, which may require reflecting back on what you've heard until you have a consensus, move on to focus on the way forward. Aim to find common ground and reach an amicable solution. Think of options together and agree on any outcomes. Proposing options helps the other person see a way out. Talk about how you would like to approach this or other issues if they were to come up again in the future.

TIPS FOR MEETINGS TO DISCUSS PROBLEMS

- Don't wait too long or until a formal meeting. Have a quiet word at the first sign that something needs to be discussed.

- Set the right tone from the start of the meeting – adopt a calm, measured, deliberate but friendly approach.

- Focus on the issue and not the person.

- Allow people to have their say and listen to them.

- Keep an open mind and don't jump to conclusions.

- Acknowledge the individual's point of view and, if it is a disciplinary issue, any mitigating circumstances.

- Discuss with the individual the options available for dealing with the situation, and if possible agree on action by the individual, the manager or jointly.

- Define the way forward if agreement cannot be reached, with reasons and explanations of any actions proposed.

TIPS FOR MEETINGS TO CONVEY BAD NEWS

- Decide how you are going to present a management decision having considered the consequences for the individual concerned.

- Explain the reason for the decision.

- Be prepared for the possibility that the individual may feel resentful or upset and react angrily or emotionally. If they are angry, allow them to let off steam but keep the meeting under control. If they react emotionally again, allow them to express their feelings and offer to arrange help where possible.

- Discuss the implications for the individual.

- Offer support when, through no fault of theirs, the individual will be adversely affected by the decision, for example help in finding another job for someone made redundant.

Political skills 31

People professionals need political skills to cope with, and indeed thrive on, the politics that are rife in most organizations. What this involves is described in this chapter under the following headings:

1 The nature of organizational politics
2 Dealing with organizational politics
3 Tips

The nature of organizational politics

Political behaviour in organizations takes place when people, probably managers or senior professionals, get their way without going through normal channels or exerting their own authority.

When acting politically people get things done by lobbying decision makers and doing deals. Other ploys include withholding information, which recognizes the fact that knowledge is power. Organizational politicians can go behind people's backs, hatch up plots in dark corners, 'sew things up' before meetings (lobbying) and exert undue influence on weaker brethren. You may not deign to practise these political black arts but it is useful to be aware of the possibility that others will so that you are prepared for that eventuality. The signs of excessive indulgence in political behaviour include:

- buck-passing;
- secret meetings and hidden decisions;
- feuds between people and departments;
- email wars between armed camps – arguing by email rather than meeting people face-to-face is a sign of distrust;
- a multiplicity of snide comments and criticisms;
- excessive and counterproductive lobbying;
- the formation of cabals – cliques that spend their time intriguing.

It can be an insidious and hidden process which subverts the rational and open approach to decision making that organizations like to think they adopt. But it can be a way of getting things done. Lobbying a colleague to persuade them to support a proposal put to a decision-making committee (they do exist) is a political act. It could be regarded as justifiable if the outcome is a worthwhile decision that might not otherwise have been made. And it can be argued that a political approach to management is inevitable in any organization where the clarity of goals is not absolute, where the decision-making process is not clear-cut and where the authority to make decisions is not evenly or appropriately distributed. There can be few organizations where one or more of these conditions do not apply.

Dealing with organizational politics

To deal with organizational politics a degree of political sensitivity is desirable – knowing what is going on so the politics affecting behaviour can be taken into account. It is necessary to understand the culture of the organization ('how things are done around here'), know how key decisions are made, who makes them and the factors that are likely to affect them. People professionals need to know where the power base is in the organization (sometimes called the 'dominant coalition') – who makes the running, who are the people who count when decisions are taken – and they should make themselves aware of what is going on behind the scenes. They have to network – identify the interest groups and keep in contact with them. They need to discover any 'hidden agendas' – try to understand what people are really getting at beneath the surface by getting answers to the question: 'Where are they coming from?'

A more positive approach to keeping politics operating at an acceptable level is for people professionals to use their influence in their organization development role to encourage the management of the organization's operations as transparently as possible. The aim should be to ensure that issues are debated fully, that differences of opinion are dealt with frankly and that disagreements are de-personalized, so far as this is possible.

TIPS

- Accept that politics are a typical characteristic of life in organizations.

- Develop 'political sensitivity' – an understanding of the main political issues in the organization, who is involved and what can be done to make the best of them.

- Identify the interest groups and people of influence (network). Get to know what they are after and bring things out into the open if you can.

- Recognize that there are occasions when you may have to take a political approach to get something done. But be careful. You may say to yourself 'the end justifies the means' but that is a dangerous doctrine if it subverts the normal transparent process of decision making.

Managing conflict

32

People professionals can be involved in resolving conflict between individuals and groups in organizations and within teams. This chapter examines this role under the following headings:

1 The nature of conflict

2 Handling inter-group conflict

3 Handling interpersonal conflict

4 Resolving conflict between team members

5 Tips

The nature of conflict

Conflict is inevitable in organizations because they function by means of adjustments and compromises among competitive elements in their structure and membership. Conflict also arises when there is change, because it may be seen as a threat to be challenged or resisted, or when there is frustration – this may produce an aggressive reaction: fight rather than flight.

Conflict is not necessarily negative and is not always to be deplored. It is bound to happen sometimes because it is part of how we build relationships. It results from progress and change and it can and should be used constructively. Being able to discuss different opinions is an essential part of healthy decision making. Bland agreement on everything would be unnatural and enervating. There should be clashes of ideas about tasks and projects, and disagreements should not be suppressed. They should come out into the open because that is the only way to ensure that the issues are explored and conflicts are resolved. It is an inevitable concomitant of progress and change. What is regrettable is failure to use conflict constructively. Effective problem solving and constructive confrontation both resolve conflicts and open up channels of discussion and cooperative action.

Many years ago, one of the pioneering and most influential writers on management, Mary Parker Follett (1924), wrote that differences can be made to contribute to the common cause if they are resolved by integration rather than domination or compromise.

In fact, organizations that spend too much time trying to avoid disagreements may well end up reaching a consensus without critical reasoning or evaluation of the consequences and alternatives, and make poorer decisions as a result. Debate, discussions and differences of opinion lead to better, more robust outcomes and greater diversity of thought.

There is such a thing as creative conflict – new or modified ideas, insights, approaches and solutions can be generated by a joint re-examination of different points of view, as long as this is based on an objective and rational exchange of information and opinions. But conflict becomes counterproductive when it is based on personality clashes, or when it is treated as an unseemly mess to be hurriedly cleared away, rather than as a problem to be worked through. Conflict resolution deals with ways of settling differences between groups, individuals and team members.

Handling inter-group conflict

There are three ways of resolving inter-group conflict: peaceful coexistence, compromise and problem solving.

Peaceful coexistence

The aim here is to smooth out differences and emphasize the common ground. People are encouraged to learn to live together, there is a good deal of information, contact and exchange of views, and individuals move freely between groups (for example, between headquarters and the field, or between sales and marketing).

This is a pleasant ideal, but it may not be practicable in some situations. There is much evidence that conflict is not necessarily resolved by simply bringing people together. There is also the danger that the real issues will be submerged for the moment in a spirit of superficial cooperation but will surface again later.

Compromise

The issue is resolved by negotiation or bargaining and neither party wins or loses. This concept of splitting the difference is essentially pessimistic. The hallmark of this approach is that there is no 'right' or 'best' answer. Agreements only accommodate differences. Real issues are unlikely to be solved.

Problem solving

An attempt is made to find a genuine solution to the problem rather than just accommodating different points of view. This is where the apparent paradox of 'creative conflict' comes in. Conflict situations can be used to advantage to create better solutions.

If solutions are to be developed by problem solving, they have to be generated by those who share the responsibility for seeing that the solutions work. The sequence of actions is: first, those concerned work through to define the problem and agree on the objectives to be attained in reaching a solution; second, the group develops alternative solutions and debates their merits; and third, agreement is reached on the preferred course of action and how it should be implemented.

Handling interpersonal conflict

Handling conflict between individuals can be more difficult than resolving conflicts between groups. Whether the conflict is openly hostile or subtly covert, strong personal feelings may be involved. However, interpersonal conflict, like inter-group conflict, is an organizational reality that is not necessarily good or bad. It can be destructive, but it can also play a productive role. The approaches to dealing with it are withdrawal, smoothing over differences, reaching a compromise, counselling and constructive confrontation.

Withdrawal

The reaction to interpersonal conflict may be the triumph of one party, leaving the other one to hold the field. This is the classic win/lose situation – a zero-sum game. Pressure may have been exerted to resolve the issue by force, but this may not be the best solution if it represents a point of view that has ignored counter-arguments and has, in fact, steamrollered over them. The winner may be triumphant but the loser will be aggrieved and either demotivated or resolved to fight again another day. There may have been a lull in the conflict but not an end to it.

Smoothing over differences

Another approach is to smooth over differences and pretend that the conflict does not exist, although no attempt has been made to tackle the root causes. Again, this is an unsatisfactory solution. The issue is likely to re-emerge and the battle will recommence.

Reaching a compromise

Yet another approach is bargaining to reach a compromise. This means that both sides are prepared to lose as well as win some points and the aim is to reach a solution acceptable to both sides. Bargaining, however, involves all sorts of tactical and often counterproductive games, and the parties are often more anxious to seek acceptable compromises than to achieve sound solutions.

Counselling

Personal counselling is an approach that does not address the conflict itself but focuses on how the two people are reacting. It gives people a chance to release pent-up tensions and may encourage them to think about new ways of resolving the conflict. But it does not address the essential nature of the conflict, which is the relationship between two people. That is why constructive confrontation offers the best hope of a long-term solution.

Constructive confrontation

Constructive confrontation is a method of bringing the individuals in conflict together. People management professionals can play a role in this process by acting as third parties, helping to build an exploratory and cooperative climate. This is highly skilled work and it is best to have training in counselling techniques.

Constructive confrontation aims to get the contending parties to understand and explore the other's perceptions and feelings. It is a process of developing mutual understanding to produce a win/win situation. The issues will be confronted but on the basis of a joint analysis, with the help of the third party, of facts relating to the situation and the actual behaviour of those involved. Feelings will be expressed but they will be analysed by reference to specific events and behaviours rather than inferences or speculations about motives. Third parties have a key role in this process, and it is not an easy one. They have to get agreement to the ground rules for discussions aimed at bringing out the facts and minimizing hostile behaviour. They must monitor the ways in which negative feelings are expressed and encourage the parties to produce new definitions of the problem and its cause or causes and new motives to reach a common solution. Third parties must avoid the temptation to support or appear to support either of those in contention. They should adopt a counselling approach, which means listening actively, observing as well as listening and helping people to understand, define and resolve the problem by asking pertinent, open-ended questions.

Resolving conflict between team members

To resolve conflict between team members the following actions can be taken:

1 Obtain an overview of the situation from your own observations.

2 Find out who is involved.

3 Talk to each of the parties to the conflict to obtain their side of the story.

4 Talk to other members of the group to get their views, being careful to be dispassionate and strictly neutral.

5 Evaluate what you hear from both parties and other people against your knowledge of what has been happening, any history of conflict and the dispositions and previous behaviour of the people involved.

6 Reach preliminary conclusions on the facts, the reasons for the dispute and the extent to which either of the parties or both of them are to blame (but keep these to yourself at this stage).

7 Bring the parties together to discuss the situation. The initial aim of this meeting would be to bring the problem out into the open, get the facts and defuse any emotions that may prejudice a solution to the problem. Both parties should be allowed to have their say but, as the facilitator of this meeting, you should do your best to ensure that they stick to the facts and explain their point of view dispassionately. You should not even remotely give the impression that you are taking sides.

8 Try to defuse the situation so that a solution can be reached that on the whole will be acceptable to all concerned. Ideally, this should be an integrated solution reached by agreement on the basis of collaboration along the lines of 'Let's get together to find the best solution on the basis of the facts'. It may be necessary to reach a compromise or accommodation – something everyone can live with.

9 Only if all else fails or the parties are so recalcitrant in holding an untenable position that no integrated, compromise or accommodating solution can be reached, should you resort to direct action – instructing one or both of the parties to bury their differences and get on with their work. If the worst comes to the worst this may involve disciplinary action, beginning with a formal warning.

TIPS

- Accept that while conflict may be inevitable in organizations, there are ways of managing it that prevent it from being destructive.

- Embrace the notion of creative conflict – that new or modified ideas, insights, approaches and solutions can be generated by a joint re-examination of the different points of view as long as this is based on an objective and rational exchange of information and ideas.

- Remember the words of Mary Parker Follett: 'Differences can be made to contribute to the common cause if they are resolved by integration rather than domination or compromise.'

- Try to find a genuine solution to the problem rather than just accommodating different points of view.

- Help people to define problems for themselves.

- Encourage people to explore alternative solutions.

- Get people to develop their own plans to deal with the conflict situation but provide advice and help if asked.

Reference

Follett, M P (1924) *Creative Experience*, New York, Longmans Green

PART SIX
Business skills

Understanding the business   33

People professionals who work in a business need to see themselves – and be seen – as business people with particular expertise and interest in people, rather than people professionals who happen to work for a business. To make an effective contribution, they must possess business and financial skills including the ability to deal with business issues from a people management perspective. This chapter is set out under the following headings:

1 The importance of understanding the business

2 Business skills

3 Financial skills

4 Business models

5 Dealing with business issues from a people management perspective

6 Tips

The importance of understanding the business

An ability to understand the business agenda means that people professionals who work in a business can develop insight into the issues and demands that affect people management. They are then in a position to help the business to achieve its objectives by factoring in those considerations. When the people management function is grounded in the business and delivering the fundamentals well it will achieve greater credibility and exert more influence. This requirement was spelt out by Ulrich (1997) when he wrote: 'HR professionals must know the business, which includes a mastery of finance, strategy, marketing, and operations'. The profession map of the CIPD (2022) states that people professionals need to know:

- their organization's business model and areas of competitive advantage, and where value is created and lost;
- how people practices create value for different stakeholders, and the associated risks;
- how to interpret their organization's performance data, identify people risks and mitigating actions;
- how to contribute to business performance by reviewing and forecasting spend and calculating return on investment.

Equipped with this knowledge, people professionals can develop the skills needed to interpret the organization's business or corporate strategies, to contribute to the formulation of those strategies, to develop integrated people management strategies and to run their own function in a business-like way.

Business skills

People management professionals who are business-like understand and act upon:

- the business imperatives of the organization – its mission and its strategic goals;
- the organization's business model – the basis upon which its business is done (how its mission and strategic goals will be achieved);
- the organization's business drivers – the characteristics of the business that move it forward;
- the organization's core competencies – what the business is good at doing;
- how performance in the organization is measured in financial and non-financial terms;
- the factors that will ensure the effectiveness of its activities including specific issues concerning profitability, productivity, financial budgeting and control, costs and benefits, customer service and operational performance;

- the importance of achieving competitive advantage through people – competitive advantage is the ability of a business to outperform competitors thus achieving and sustaining better results than rivals and placing the firm in a competitive position;
- the factors that will ensure that the firm's resources, especially its people, create sustained competitive advantage because they are valuable, imperfectly imitable and non-substitutable (the resource-based view);
- the key performance indicators (KPIs) of the business (the results or outcomes identified as being crucial to the achievement of high performance) that can be used to measure progress towards attaining goals.

Financial skills

A business-like approach means using financial skills to know how to analyse and interpret balance sheets, cash flow and trading statements and profit and loss accounts, and to understand and make use of the financial techniques of budgeting and budgetary control, cash budgeting and costing.

Interpreting balance sheets

A balance sheet is a statement on the last day of the accounting period of the company's assets and liabilities and the share capital or the shareholders' investment in the company. Balance sheet analysis assesses the financial strengths and weaknesses of the company, primarily from the point of view of the shareholders and potential investors, but also as part of management's task to exercise proper stewardship over the funds invested in the company and the assets in its care. With the help of balance sheet ratios, the analysis focuses on the balance sheet equation, considers the make-up of the balance sheet in terms of assets and liabilities, and examines the liquidity position (how much cash or easily realizable assets are available) and capital structure.

The balance sheet equation

The balance sheet equation is: Capital + Liabilities = Assets. Capital plus liabilities shows where the money comes from, and assets indicates where the money is now.

Make-up of the balance sheet

The balance sheet contains four major sections:

- *Assets or capital in use*, which is divided into long-term or fixed assets (e.g. land, buildings and plant) and current or short-term assets, which include bank balances and cash, debtors, stocks of goods and materials, and work in progress.

- *Current liabilities*, which are the amounts that will have to be paid within 12 months of the balance sheet date.

- *Net current assets or working capital*, which are current assets less current liabilities. Careful control of working capital lies at the heart of efficient business performance.

- *Sources of capital*, which comprise share capital, reserves including retained profits, and long-term loans.

Liquidity analysis

Liquidity analysis is concerned with the extent to which the organization has an acceptable quantity of cash and easily realizable assets to meet its needs. The analysis may be based on the ratio of current assets (cash, working capital, etc) to current liabilities (the working capital ratio). Too low a ratio may mean that the liquid resources are insufficient to cover short-term payments. Too high a ratio might indicate that there is too much cash or working capital and that they are therefore being badly managed. The working capital ratio is susceptible to 'window dressing', which is the manipulation of the working capital position by accelerating or delaying transactions near the year-end.

Liquidity analysis also uses the 'quick ratio' of current assets minus stocks to current liabilities. This concentrates on the more realizable of the current assets and therefore provides a stricter test of liquidity than the working capital ratio. It is therefore called 'the acid test'.

Capital structure analysis

Capital structure analysis examines the overall means by which a company finances its operations, which is partly by the funds of their ordinary shareholders (equity) and partly by loans from banks and other lenders (debt). The ratio of long-term debt to ordinary shareholders' funds indicates 'gearing'. A company is said to be highly geared when it has a high level of loan capital as distinct from equity capital.

Classification of profits

Profit is basically the amount by which revenues exceed costs. It is classified in trading statements and profit and loss accounts in the following four ways:

1 *Gross profit* – the difference between sales revenue and the cost of goods sold. This is also referred to as gross margin, especially in the retail industry.
2 *Operating or trading profit* – the gross profit less sales, marketing and distribution costs, administrative costs and research and development expenditure.
3 *Profit before taxation* – operating profit plus invested income minus interest payable.
4 *Net profit* – profit minus taxation.

Trading statements

Trading statements or accounts show the cost of goods manufactured, the cost of sales, sales revenue and the gross profit, which is transferred to the profit and loss account.

Profit and loss accounts

Profit and loss accounts provide the information required to assess a company's profitability – the return in the shape of profits that shareholders obtain for their investment in the company. This is the primary aim and best measure of efficiency in a competitive business. Profit and loss accounts show:

1 The gross profit from the trading account.
2 Selling and administration expenses.
3 The operating profit (1 minus 2).
4 Investment income.
5 Profit before interest and taxation (3 plus 4).
6 Profit before taxation (5 minus loan interest).
7 Taxation.
8 Net profit (6 minus 7).

Profitability analysis ratios

Profitability is expressed by the following ratios:

- *Return on equity* – profit after interest and preference dividends before tax in relation to ordinary share capital, reserves and retained profit. This focuses attention on the efficiency of the company in earning profits on behalf of its shareholders; some analysts regard it as the best profitability ratio.

- *Return on capital employed* – trading or operating profit to capital employed. This measures the efficiency with which capital is employed.

- *Earnings per share* – profit after interest, taxation and preference dividends in relation to the number of issued ordinary shares. This is an alternative to return on equity as a measure of the generation of 'shareholder value' (the value of the investment made by shareholders in the company in terms of the return they get on that investment). Its drawback is that it depends on the number of shares issued, although it is often referred to within companies as the means by which their obligations to shareholders should be assessed.

- *Price-earnings (P/E) ratio* – market price of ordinary shares in relation to earnings per share. This ratio is often used by investment analysts.

- *Economic value added (EVA)* – post-tax operating profit minus the cost of capital invested in the business. This measures how effectively the company uses its funds.

Financial budgeting

Budgets translate policy into financial terms. They are statements of the planned allocation and use of the company's financial resources. They are needed to: 1) show the financial implications of plans, 2) define the resources required to achieve the plans, and 3) provide the means of measuring, monitoring and controlling results against the plans. People professionals need to know how budgets should be prepared and controlled.

The procedure for preparing financial budgets consists of the following steps:

1 *Budget guidelines* are prepared that have been derived from the corporate plan and forecasts. They will include the activity levels for which budgets have to be created and the ratios to be achieved. The assumptions to be used in budgeting are also given. These could include rates of inflation and increases in costs and prices.

2 *Initial budgets* for a budget or cost centre are prepared by departmental managers with the help of budget accountants.

3 *Departmental budgets* are collated and analysed to produce the master budget, which is reviewed by top management, who may require changes at departmental level to bring it into line with corporate financial objectives and plans.

4 *The master budget* is finally approved by top management and issued to each departmental (budget centre) manager for planning and control purposes.

Budgetary control

Budgetary control ensures that financial budgets are met and that any variances are identified and dealt with. Control starts with the budget for the cost centre, which sets out the budgeted expenditure under cost headings against activity levels. A system of measurement or recording is used to allocate expenditures to cost headings and record activity levels achieved. The actual expenditures and activity levels are compared and positive and negative variances noted. Cost centre managers then act to deal with the variances and report their results to higher management. Heads of people functions need to understand how they should monitor and control expenditure.

Cash management

Cash management involves forecasting and controlling cash flows (inflows or outflows of cash to or from the company). It is an important and systematic process of ensuring that problems of cash liquidity are minimized and that funds are managed effectively. The aim is to ensure that the company is not over-trading, i.e. that the cost of its operations does not significantly exceed the amount of cash available to finance them. The old adage is that whatever else is done, ensure that 'cash in exceeds cash out'.

Cash flow statements report the amounts of cash generated and cash used for a period. They are used to provide information on liquidity (the availability of cash), solvency and financial adaptability.

Cash budgeting

An operating cash budget deals with budgeted receipts (forecast cash inflows) and budgeted payments (forecast cash outflows). It includes all the revenue expenditure incurred in financing current operations, i.e. the costs of running the business in order to generate sales.

Costing

Costing techniques provide information for decision making and control. They are used to establish the total cost of a product for stock valuation, pricing and estimating purposes and to enable the company to establish that the proposed selling price will enable a profit to be made.

Costing involves measuring the direct costs of material and labour plus the indirect costs (overheads) originating in the factory (factory overheads) and elsewhere in the company (sales, distribution, marketing, research and development and administration). Overheads are charged to cost units – this process is called 'overhead recovery'. It provides information on total costs. Costing has to take account of fixed costs, which do not vary with activity levels, and variable costs, which do. There are four main costing methods:

- *Absorption costing* – this involves allocating all fixed and variable costs to cost units and is the most widely used method, although it can be arbitrary.

- *Activity-based costing* – costs are assigned to activities on the basis of an individual product's demand for each activity.

- *Marginal costing* – this segregates fixed costs and apportions the variable or marginal costs to products.

- *Standard costing* – the preparation of predetermined or standard costs, which are compared with actual costs to identify variances. It is used to measure performance.

Business models

People professionals need to know about the concept of business models and how this influences their activities. A business model provides a picture of an organization, explaining how it achieves competitive advantage. As defined by Magretta (2002), business models:

> … are at heart stories – stories that explain how enterprises work… They answer the fundamental questions every manager needs to ask: How do we make money in this business? What is the underlying economic logic that explains how we can deliver value to customers at an appropriate cost?

She explained that a business model 'focuses attention on how all the elements in a system fit into a working whole'.

Elements of a business model

The elements of a business model that, taken together, create and deliver value are:

- *The customer value proposition*: how the business will create value for its customers; this is the most important element.
- *The profit formula*: the blueprint that defines how the company creates value for itself while providing value to the customer. It consists of the revenue model, cost structure, margin model (the contribution needed from each transaction to achieve desired profits) and resource velocity (the ratio of the value of the goods the company produces and sells or the services it provides to the value of the investment in producing or delivering those goods or services over the same period of time). It is also concerned with how fast the business needs to turn over inventory and assets and how well resources should be utilized. Inventory or stock refers to the goods and materials that a business holds; inventory or stock turnover measures the number of times inventory is sold or used in a time period. It is calculated to see if a business has an excessive inventory in comparison to its sales level.

Business model innovation

Business model innovation is the process of developing new ways of doing business or changing existing ones in order to deliver better value to customers, achieve competitive advantage and increase profitability.

The basis of business model innovation is business model analysis, which is concerned with: 1) how the organization creates value, and 2) how the organization establishes unique resources, assets or positions that will achieve competitive advantage. It may involve an analysis of how value is generated at each stage of the value chain (a value chain consists of the sequence of activities in a firm that are strategically relevant and underlie its key capabilities). Value is created in a number of ways but, clearly, the contribution of people is vital.

The role of people management in business model innovation

To play their part in business model innovation, people professionals need to:

- understand the implications of the existing and potential business model in terms of the organization structure and the new or enhanced capabilities the people involved will require;

- contribute to the redesign of the organization to meet the requirements of the business model change programme;

- plan organization development activities that systematically improve organizational capability in terms of process – how things get done;

- mastermind change management programmes that provide for the acceptance and smooth implementation of change;

- conduct workforce planning exercises that identify more specifically the numbers of people required with specified skills and knowledge;

- formulate and implement talent management strategies that provide for the development, deployment, recruitment and retention of talented people – those individuals who can make a difference to organizational performance through their immediate contribution and in the longer term;

- develop performance-driven processes such as skills development programmes, performance management and performance pay;

- ensure that people have the skills required to implement the new or changed business model;

- establish knowledge management procedures for storing and sharing the wisdom, understanding and expertise accumulated in the organization about its processes, techniques and operations.

In addition, as Schuler and Jackson (2007) pointed out, 'Because an innovation strategy requires risk taking and tolerance of inevitable failures, HRM in firms pursuing this strategy should be used to give employees a sense of security and encourage a long-term commitment'.

Dealing with business issues from a people management perspective

People professionals have to deal with business issues from a people management perspective. They must also be able to identify the business issues that influence how it operates and how the people in the business are treated. These include performance generally, productivity, quality, sales and customer service.

To deal with a business issue:

- define the nature of the issue – what is involved, who is involved, what impact it is it having on organizational performance and on the wellbeing of employees;

- analyse the extent to which the issue is caused by some aspect of how the business is functioning or responding to events or by some people factor;

- consider what can be done immediately to mitigate the impact on employees, particularly the possibility of redundancy or a fire-and-rehire proposal;

- consider what can be done in the longer term to improve performance and productivity;

- persuade management to accept the short- and long-term proposals with convincing arguments on their likely success and reminders of the potential reputational damage that may result from drastic actions.

TIPS

- Develop and use business and financial skills to provide a basis for integrated people management strategies – ones that are aligned to business strategies and thus help to achieve them.

- Get to know what the business model of the organization is – how the organization delivers value to its customers and, in commercial organizations, how the business achieves competitive advantage and makes money.

- Track the financial performance of the business as shown in balance sheets etc. and use this information to reinforce the need for performance-enhancing people management activities.

- Identify the people implications of business issues.
- Make recommendations based on costed options and develop and present a persuasive business case for proposals.

References

CIPD (2022) Profession Map, https://www.cipd.org/globalassets/media/comms/the-people-profession/profession-map-pdfs/profession-map_full-standards-download.pdf (archived at https://perma.cc/77KU-DV6Z)

Magretta, J (2002) Why business models matter, *Harvard Business Review*, May, pp 86–93

Schuler, R S and Jackson, S E (2007) *Strategic Human Resource Management, 2nd edition*, Wiley, Oxford

Ulrich, D (1997) Judge me by my future not my past, *Human Resource Management*, **36** (1), pp 5–8

Enhancing performance skills

34

People professionals can play an important part in helping to improve the level of performance in an organization. This role is examined in this chapter under the following headings:

1 The role of people professionals as performance consultants

2 Performance enhancement interventions

3 Tips

The role of people professionals as performance consultants

Performance consulting is the process of identifying or responding to a business need to improve performance, analysing the nature of the need and the reasons for it, possibly using a diagnostic, and deciding what contribution the people function could make to satisfying the need. This means advising on initiatives such as smart working which affect the way in which work is organized, or proposing people management interventions such as performance management that are designed to make a direct impact on individual or team performance.

Performance consultants can use a diagnostic devised by Weisbord (1976), which he called the Six Boxes Model. Information is collected and analysed under the following six headings to identify and deal with behavioural problems that negatively affect performance:

1 Expectations and feedback

2 Tools and resources

3 Consequences

4 Skills and knowledge

5 Selection and assignment (capacity)

6 Motives and preferences (attitude)

To be effective as performance consultants, people professionals need to possess business acumen and know the key factors that affect organizational performance. They have to understand how these factors impinge on the performance expected from individual employees. They also need the skills required to advise on or develop the performance improvement interventions described below.

Performance enhancement interventions

The interventions aiming to directly lead to performance improvements are smart or agile working, high-performance work systems, performance management, performance-related pay and skills development. People professionals need high levels of skill to be able to contribute to the development of any of these.

Smart working

The characteristics of smart, sometimes called 'agile' working are:

- flexibility in work locations and hours;
- self-management – a high degree of autonomy and a philosophy of empowerment;
- the use of virtual teams;
- focus on outcome-based indicators of performance;
- high-performance working;
- use of more advanced communications technology;
- hot-desking;
- the development of high-trust working relationships;
- alignment of smart working with business objectives.

High-performance work systems

High-performance work systems are designed to encourage continuing high levels of performance. Their features vary according to the context but typically they will include:

- *Job infrastructure* – workplace arrangements that equip workers with the proper abilities to do their jobs, provide them with the means to do their jobs, and give them the motivation to do their jobs. These practices must be combined to produce their proper effects.
- *Training programmes to enhance employee skills* – investment in increasing employee skills, knowledge and ability.
- *Information-sharing and worker involvement mechanisms* – to understand the available alternatives and make correct decisions.
- *Reward and promotion opportunities that provide motivation* – to encourage skilled employees to engage in effective discretionary decision making in a variety of environmental contingencies.

This is an integrated method of people management which requires considerable skills to develop and maintain. People professionals may decide to adopt an incremental approach, prioritizing the interventions on their potential impact and also on the ease with which they can be introduced

Performance management

Traditionally, people managers needed the skills required to develop and administrate formal performance management systems. But these are being replaced by a less formal approach which focuses on getting line managers to act as 'performance leaders', meaning that they rely on frequent 'performance conversations' with their staff that adopt a much more informal way of talking about successes (to encourage continuing high levels of performance) and areas for improvement (to overcome performance problems). But this approach makes considerable demands on line managers and people professionals have an important and skilled role in providing advice and guidance on how they should do it.

Performance-related pay

Schemes aimed at motivating people by relating pay to levels of performance (PRP schemes) are one of the two most used people management initiatives designed to enhance performance. The other is performance management. But considerable skill is required to develop and operate a scheme that has that effect. Many fail and some even demotivate people because they operate unfairly.

Skills development

Skills development starts with the identification of skills development requirements. This is done by establishing from workforce plans what types of skills will be wanted to meet strategic objectives, conducting an analysis of what skills are available, identifying any skill gaps, finding out if there are any organizational problems that could be attributed to skills shortages or deficiencies, and noting any indication from performance review reports of individual skills problems. Plans can then be made for filling gaps and remedying deficiencies through formal training programmes, encouraging line managers to be more involved in training their staff and facilitating self-development activities on the part of employees.

TIPS

- Keep an eye on performance and productivity levels to indicate where special action might be necessary.

- Consider the alternatives, bearing in mind that none of them is easy.

- Assess which alternative is most likely to fit the needs and circumstances of the organization and its employees and will not be too hard to manage.

- Prepare a proposal that convincingly sets out the benefits of the suggested initiative.

- If the proposal is accepted, organize and operate a development and implementation project.

Reference

Weisbord, M R (1976) Organizational diagnosis: six places to look for trouble with or without a theory, *Group Organization Management*, **1**, pp 430–47

Administrative skills   35

The skills required by people professionals to administrate their work are examined in this chapter under the following headings:

1 The nature of administration in people management

2 The administrative skills required

3 Tips

The nature of administration in people management

Administration is defined as the process of providing for the smooth running of an operational activity in an organization. It involves defining the purpose of the activity, planning for how it is to take place, providing the resources required and seeing that the activity is carried out efficiently and as planned. It means carrying out or supervising the administrative tasks of prioritizing, scheduling, getting things done on time, recording, analysing, communicating and reporting.

Administration may not be the most glamorous aspect of a people professional's job but it is an important one. In a sense, people professionals are in the delivery business. They offer strategic advice and advise on key people issues but they are also there to provide the services expected by their clients – senior management and line managers. And this means that they have to run those people management services efficiently. The reputation of the people management function will be damaged if they don't. You can be as strategic as you like but it won't do you any good if you don't deliver the goods.

The areas of people management in which administration takes place are many and varied. They include:

- maintaining the database of information about employees;
- running the payroll;

- developing the use of digital people management, including the application of artificial intelligence and ChatGPT or similar systems;
- planning and conducting recruitment campaigns and talent management programmes;
- organizing learning and development programmes;
- operating performance management and reward management systems;
- managing the provision of employee benefits and pensions, including the organization of flexible benefit schemes;
- health and safety management;
- providing wellbeing facilities for employees including employee assistance programmes and arrangements for financial wellbeing;
- managing various operations or facilities which may be placed under the control of the people management function acting in an administrative capacity for want of anywhere else to put them; these include restaurant and canteen facilities, the car fleet, a social enterprise network, the organization of events such as social gatherings for employees and 'away days' (management conferences held outside the firm).

The administrative skills required

A variety of administrative skills are required to complete these administrative tasks. These were exemplified in *Summer Lightning* by P G Wodehouse, in which he dubs Lord Emsworth's secretary 'the efficient Baxter' and explains:

> We have called Rupert Baxter efficient and efficient he was. The word as we interpret it, implies not only a capacity for performing the ordinary tasks of life with a smooth firmness of touch, but in addition, a certain alertness of mind, a genius for opportunism, a genius for seeing clearly, thinking swiftly and Doing it Now.

In addition to these qualities, people professionals need to be methodical. They must be able to do things carefully, systematically and thoroughly, and in a well-ordered, structured and business-like way. Because they have to multi-task, they have to be good at prioritizing. And because the range of tasks may be considerable, they have to be adaptable – able to adjust their approach to the different demands of each of their administrative tasks.

TIPS

- Remember that while administration means doing things right (being efficient) it also involves doing the right thing (being effective). Don't allow the natural wish for everything to function smoothly and according to plan to become a bureaucratic exercise; always focus on the end results required.

- Manage your time carefully – you don't want to admit, like Richard II in Shakespeare's play: 'I wasted time but time has wasted me.'

- Plan and organize administrative activities with care but be prepared to adapt your approach if circumstances change, which they will. Remember Murphy's law: 'If anything can go wrong, it will.'

- In the words of Theodore Roosevelt: 'Do what you can, with what you have, where you are.'

- Control the administrative activity by planning what has to be achieved, measuring or assessing regularly what *has* been achieved, comparing actual achievements with the plan, and taking any actions to correct deviations from the plan.

- Prioritize by (1) deciding on the relative importance of the administrative tasks that have to be done – an obvious example would be to place a request for information from your CEO at the top of the list; (2) assessing the urgency of the task – what will happen if a deadline is not met; and (3) considering how best to make use of the time available.

Reference

Wodehouse, P G (1029) *Summer Lightning*, paperback edition by Penguin Classics (Harmondsworth)

Project management skills

36

People management professionals are often called upon to manage or take part in projects such as developing a new performance management system or job evaluation scheme, setting up a new learning centre or revising a pay structure. They therefore need project management skills as described in this chapter under the following headings:

1 The nature of project management

2 Project planning

3 Setting up the project

4 Controlling the project

5 Tips

The nature of project management

Project management is the planning, supervision and control of any activity or set of activities that leads to a defined outcome at a predetermined time, in accordance with specified performance or quality standards and at a budgeted cost. It is concerned with *deliverables* – getting things done as required or promised. While delivering results on time is important, it is equally important to deliver them to meet the specification and within the projected cost.

Project planning

Project management starts with action planning – deciding *what* work is to be done, *why* the work needs to be done, *who* will do the work, *how much* it will cost, *when* it has to be completed (totally or stage by stage) and *where* it will be carried out.

Initiation

The first step is to define the objectives of the project. A business case has to be made. This means answering two basic questions:

1 Why is this project needed?
2 What benefits are expected from the project?

Assessment

Projects mean investing resources – money and people. Investment appraisal techniques may be used to ensure that the company's criteria on return on investment are satisfied. Cost-benefit analysis may be used to assess the degree to which the benefits justify the costs, time and number of people required by the project. This may mean identifying opportunity costs that establish whether a greater benefit would be obtained by investing the money or deploying the people on other projects or activities.

Performance specification

This sets out what the project is expected to do – how it should perform – and describes the details of the project's configuration or method of operation.

Project plan

The project plan sets out:

- the major activities in sequence – the stages of the project;
- a breakdown where appropriate of each major operation into a sequence of subsidiary tasks;

- the time required to complete each major operation or stage;
- an assessment of the resources required – money, people and equipment;
- a cost budget for the project as a whole broken down into each main activity and stage;
- how many people will be allocated to the project with different skills at each stage;
- who is to be responsible for controlling the project as a whole and at each of the major stages or operations.

Setting up the project

Setting up the project involves:

- selecting and briefing the project management team;
- obtaining and allocating resources;
- finalizing the programme – defining each stage;
- establishing control systems, especially those concerned with controlling the cost budget and the progress of the project against the plan;
- defining reporting procedures (format and timing of progress reports);
- identifying key dates, stage by stage, for the project (milestones) and providing for milestone meetings to review progress and decide on any actions required.

Controlling the project

The three most important things to control are:

1 *Time* – achievement of project plan as programmed.
2 *Quality* – achievement of project specifications.
3 *Cost* – containment of costs within budget.

Project control is based on progress reports showing what is being achieved against the plan. The planned completion date, actual achievement and forecast completion date for each stage or operation are provided. The likelihood of delays, overruns or bottlenecks is thus established so that corrective action can be taken in good time.

Progress meetings should be held at predetermined intervals. These can be treated as 'milestone' meetings when they are timed to coincide with the key stages of the project.

TIPS

- Be certain about what should be done, what resources are required, who does what, when it should be done and how much it should cost.
- Ensure that everyone knows what is expected of them and has the resources to do it.
- Monitor progress continually against the plan through regular reports and at formal meetings.
- Pay particular attention to progress against the programme schedule and to costs against the project budget.
- Take swift corrective action as required, for example by reallocating resources.
- Evaluate the end result against the objectives and deliverables.

INDEX

Looking for another book?

Explore our award-winning
books from global business
experts in Human Resources,
Learning and Development

Scan the code to browse

www.koganpage.com/hr-learning-
development

Also from Kogan Page

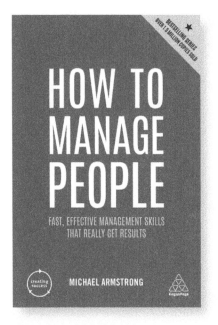

ISBN: 9781398605466

ISBN: 9781398612556

ISBN: 9781398610040

www.koganpage.com

Printed in the USA
CPSIA information can be obtained
at www.ICGtesting.com
JSHW071642060624
64414JS00010B/193